CW01646879

BLACK CHRISTIAN AND SINGLE

A collection of essays about singleness in Britain's Black Pentecostal churches

Edited by Marcia Dixon

Foreword by Dr Carol Tomlin

MTD PUBLISHING

Black, Christian and Single

First edition printed in 2022 in the United Kingdom

Publisher: MTD Publishing

Text: Ganel Simms, Joan B St Louis, Joy Adams, Ola Nubi, Andrea Best, Jeũanita Swaby, Zina Arinze, Roney Henderson, Shenelle Markland, Cherlene Wilson, Shermara Fletcher, Andrina Davis, Theresa Beckles, Belinda Smith, A A Jones, Pastor Dave Daniel

Editor: Marcia Dixon

Cover designed by: Mark Craven of eyemultimedia

Sub Editor: Jackie Raymond

A CIP catalogue record of this book is available from the British Library.

ISBN: 9781739153106

Disclaimer:

This is a collection of stories by a diverse group of people. The views expressed are those held by each individual writer and not necessarily those of Marcia Dixon MBE or the other authors included in this collection.

REVIEWS OF *BLACK, CHRISTIAN AND SINGLE*

I cannot imagine how challenging it must have been to distil the experiences of Black Christian single women, but I do know that Marcia Dixon has done it with a finesse only a talented editor like she could. With an unapologetically realistic delivery packed with emotion, *Black, Christian and Single* is a crucially important portrayal of not just the challenges faced by single women in the Church, but also how to navigate them and remain committed in the faith. Being single comes with many hurdles, but this anthology shows us there is hope amid the darkness and we should never give up.

If you have ever wondered what it was like to walk in a *Black, Christian and Single* woman's shoes, then I feel like this is an unflinchingly honest place to start.

Sanchia Alasia, HR & Diversity Specialist and Motivational Speaker

Singleness within the global Christian community still remains a taboo subject matter. Women in some instances are still treated as 'second class citizens', with marriage viewed as the ultimate life achievement. This collection of essays is brilliantly written, and addresses this issue head on, with encouragement, making this a must-read book– regardless of of relationship status.

Tobi Olujinmi, Media Producer, International Public Speaker

Black, Christian and Single is a rich tapestry of women's experiences of dating, waiting and navigating singleness in the Black UK Church. From millennial to mature, divorced or dating, searching for love or settled in celibacy, this collection of essays platforms the voices of Black Christian women who are living the challenging reality of singleness in the Church. There are many helpful tools for women in similar life circumstances, with insights from two men too! And yet Black Christian and Single goes further; it provides a wake-up call to the Church at large, and leadership in particular, to listen to and proactively support single women, especially those who desire to be married.

Clare Williams, Founder, Get Real

FOREWORD

Singleness is a hot topic in many churches in Britain and indeed around the world. The preponderance of single women in the Church is hugely concerning — particularly in British Caribbean churches, where conservative figures state there are 20 women for every man. There was a time when meeting a potential mate was relatively easy, but modern living has meant that the potential for meeting someone naturally through friends, family and in the workplace has increasingly become more complex.

Very often, when we think of singleness, the image of a woman who has never been married immediately comes to mind. Some individuals who are divorced, widowed or single parents — typically mothers — are also single. Each individual who fits into any of these categories has unique needs, so we need to be sensitive to these differences in the singleness profile.

From a Christian point of view, the Apostle Paul explained in 2 Corinthians 7 that singleness is a gift from the Lord. During the New Testament period, singleness and celibacy were actually encouraged. Paul wasn't the only one who saw singleness in a positive light. Interestingly, he was also a realist when he proclaimed it is better to marry than 'burn with passion'. He understood that marriage is the context for individuals to express their love intimately.

I would like to add that when I say 'Black', I am referring to people in the UK from the African and Caribbean communities. In many African cultures, marriage is the norm, and the eminent theologian, John Mbiti, asserted that singleness is rare in traditional African cultures. I had the pleasure of attending a predominantly West African church and everyone was expected to marry, regardless of age. Indeed, African churches in general vigorously promote marriage. However, anecdotal evidence suggests that African churches in the UK are also beginning to experience a decline in marriages. Furthermore, it isn't unusual for married couples to be separated by continents, as some men return to Africa for economic reasons, thus leaving women alone. The stresses and strain of western living have meant that some African women are single voluntarily.

Conversely, the disruption of the family unit among Black people in the Caribbean and the Americas during the slavery era has had far-reaching consequences. It has unfortunately negatively impacted gendered relationships both inside and outside the Church. Singleness is not only a challenge for women who wish to be married; the increasing number of men over 40 and unmarried in the British Caribbean community — including the Church — is also a concern. The unnatural conflict between Black men and women based on racial stereotypes, which has a long history on both sides of the Atlantic, is equally significant. Though the Windrush generation, particularly in the Church, got married, they came from a social context where, historically, many people never entered holy matrimony. For those who *did* marry, there were often 'outside children' from previous relationships.

As a British Caribbean woman who grew up in a Pentecostal church, it was common to hear ministers say: "Not everyone will get married" - invariably aimed at women. My question is, why not? Or rather, why *shouldn't* everyone or, should I say, most people who desire to be married, not be so? Perhaps we should change our language to a more hope-filled and faith-filled one. If someone is unwell, we would never say in Pentecostal/Charismatic circles "Not everyone will be healed", even if individuals are to receive their healing on the other side of eternity. We need a divine revelation and a divine strategy so that women, primarily, are provided with opportunities to be fulfilled in their godly roles as wives and mothers.

Yes, not everyone wants to be married, and some individuals — including men — are very content to be single. Still, from speaking and counselling scores of women, the vast majority do not wish to be confined to a perpetual state of singleness. In the Church, however, this appears to be their fate. I am not convinced this is the

Lord's will, however. On the contrary, God created marriage and the family, comprising man, woman and children. He wanted an extended family, the reason why He created human beings.

Many Black-Majority churches are presently filled with women and, in many cases, older women. As a matter of urgency and importance, church leaders must arise and engage with the issue of singleness: spiritually, through corporate prayer and fasting; intellectually, to gain an in-depth understanding of the situation; and practically, through strategies that will attract more men into our congregations for the well-being of single parishioners, and the future survival of our churches.

As you delve into the pages of this anthology, I pray singles will be inspired and encouraged, for you are not alone. I pray ministers will further support single members in negotiating their single state.

I would like to end with a message of hope: Live life to the full. There is no shortage of single men and women. There are over seven billion people on planet Earth, so let us go forth and expand the Kingdom of God!

Apostle Dr Carol Tomlin
Senior Apostolic Leader, Restoration Fellowship Ministries
Principal of Kingdom School of Theology
Visiting Fellow, University of Leeds

ACKNOWLEDGEMENTS

I want to thank my Lord and Saviour Jesus Christ for His grace and directing my life.

Thank you to my family for supporting me through thick and thin.

Thank you to my good long-time friend Juliet Coley for pushing and encouraging me to step up and write a book instead of just writing articles and Facebook posts!!!

Thank you to the pioneers of Britain's Black Christian Church movement. Due to their faithfulness in following God's call on their life to preach the Gospel, my life has been transformed, and I too am now a servant of God.

Thank you to everyone who has inspired, encouraged and shared their wisdom with me as I've journeyed in life.

Thank you to the writers who have shared their thoughts and experiences in *Black Christian and Single* with the aim to encourage, enlighten, inform and uplift the large numbers of single people within the Black Pentecostal Church.

INTRODUCTION

When Black Christian women get together there's one topic that is sure to get them talking: the large numbers of single women in Britain's Black Pentecostal churches and the difficulty some experience finding a life partner.

I served as editor of the Soul Stirrings column for *The Voice* newspaper for many years, and the articles that generated the most responses were those about love, sex and marriage, particularly those relating to being single. I get the same responses on social media.

My Facebook page has become known amongst my social media community as a place to discuss topical issues, and whenever I post about the difficulties Black Christian women face finding a life partner, I get *hundreds* of responses, as people are quick to share their views, experiences and solutions to what is a major point of concern for many.

The opinions expressed on my Facebook page, plus the many discussions I have been privy to over the years about singleness in the Black Church in Britain — whether on Zoom, via WhatsApp, online or face to face — have provided the inspiration for this book.

I thought it would be a beneficial project to bring together the voices of Black Christians and ask them to write about their experiences of being single — whether from a personal, professional or ministerial perspective — and put them into a book. *Black, Christian and Single* is the result.

Britain's Black Pentecostal churches are a towering legacy of the Windrush Generation. They were started by the men and women from the Caribbean who migrated *en masse* to the UK in response to the invitation by the British government to come and work in its labour-starved industries between 1948 and 1971.

Many of those migrants came here full of faith. Some had found faith in traditional denominations — like Anglican churches — in their native islands. Others were already part of the Pentecostal church movement and, when they arrived in Britain, went on a mission to plant churches that served as a place where their fellow migrants could meet with others, hear the Gospel, and get spiritual encouragement and support from other believers as they built a life in Britain.

Those churches have thrived — some are now mega churches — and also continue to provide biblical teaching, as well as empower their members to succeed in the wider world.

The message and ethos of Black Pentecostal churches have, for a variety of reasons, been particularly appealing to women, resulting in the gender imbalance. In some churches, the female/male ratio can be as high as eight to one, particularly in churches that have their roots in the Caribbean community.

A by-product of this gender imbalance within the Church has been the large numbers of single women who have been unable to find life partners.

One contributor to *Black, Christian and Single* has described much of the singleness within the Church as 'enforced singleness'. They've used the term to signify the fact there are numerous Christian women who would love to get married but haven't due to the difficulty they experience in finding someone who shares a similar faith and values.

The views and experiences of ordinary Christians on the topic of singleness aren't always heard. *Black, Christian and Single* gives the reader an opportunity to get an insight into their thoughts and experiences on this issue.

This book contains the voices of women — and a few men (two to be exact!) — and, for some contributors to this anthology, this is the first time they have ever had their writing published.

You'll hear the voices of the young, mature and wiser women sharing their first-hand accounts and observations on the broad range of issues and experiences that come under the umbrella of being Black, Christian and single. Words of encouragement and advice are offered too.

The perspectives featured in this book are many and varied. Therapist **Belinda Smith** shares how 'enforced singleness' impacts an individual's emotional health and mental well-being, and the role therapy can play in helping people find spiritual wholeness as well as the love they desire.

Coach and mentor **Zina Arinze** writes about being single from a divorced perspective, whilst **Roney Henderson** and **Theresa Beckles** shed insight into church teachings and attitudes about relationships from the '80s and '90s, and how they affected the ability of some Christians to get a date, let alone find a lifelong partner.

Joan St Louis shares how single people can lead a full life and fulfil God's purpose, even when once-held dreams of marriage are not met, and young contributors write of the positive aspects of the single life.

Cherlene Wilson writes about sex and abstinence and why, although it's difficult, refraining from sex has positive benefits, and **Pastor Dave Daniel** shares how he dealt with enforced singleness within his congregation and, in the process, saw the numbers of marriages increase.

Black, Christian and Single will make you laugh, cry, sigh, nod your head in agreement, encourage you, and possibly make you go "Oh no…" It will shed some light on why there are so many single women within the Black Church and provide some solutions on how to combat the issue.

Hope you enjoy.

Marcia Dixon MBE
Editor, *Black, Christian and Single*

CONTENTS

A LETTER TO MY SINGLE SISTERS

by Ganel Simms

Dear Single Sister

Before I share my thoughts about being single and a Christian, I want to remind you that you are blessed, and to inspire you to be courageous. I'd like to honour the woman who has accomplished great things in her career, the woman who is flourishing and constantly discovering her God-given gifts and ministry, who is a wise mother, an overcomer, and who is always supporting others to achieve great things and be the best they can be — all whilst not feeling accomplished in her desire for marriage and at times possibly feeling disappointed in God.

It is an honourable thing to desire marriage. It is one of the highest ways we can demonstrate our obedience to God, because in our romantic relationships — namely marriage — there is a demonstration of faith, hope, love and commitment. These are all qualities that not only please the Lord, but also shed light on the darkness in our world, where we can often see hopelessness, brokenness, disloyalty to God and to one another, and a lack of faithfulness.

Being unmarried is a blessing… and being married is a blessing also. The lenses we wear in each season of our lives cause us to view ourselves from many angles and perspectives. Whatever your status as a woman, whether unmarried, married or challenged in many ways, I would like to talk to you about these three things: the idol, the marriage and the self.

The Idol

As a single woman, one of the greatest challenges I have faced is acknowledging an idol in my life and having the courage to tear that idol down. An idol is an image or representation of a god, used as an object to worship. It can also be a person or thing greatly admired, loved or revered. I submit to you that there should only be one person enthroned in the life of a human being, and that is God. He is both a mystery and a revelation. He should be the constant pursuit of our hearts, and the One we admire in such a way as to 'idolise'.

An idol I had to address in my journey of singleness was the image of what a woman should have achieved by a certain age, namely: the education, the career, the car, the great social life, the house, and the husband and children, whilst also powerfully flowing in their calling of God. However, the Lord gently addressed the condition of my heart's desires one by one (and continues to, as I mature as a woman). The Lord enlightened my understanding of who I was apart from those images, and that was grave. God created us to be affirmed and validated, but not by people and things. I have been stripped of many things over the years, in order to ensure my foundation was not based upon an image that would be popular one year and unpopular the next.

I believe many women — both single and married — battle with an idol at one point or another in their lives, and this is entitled 'the image of a thing'. From my experience and from conversations with many female, married friends, though blessed to be married, the image of marriage is not what they expected when they were single.

For my peers now living as married women, the reality often fails to live up to that image, and this means some sort of compromise had to take place in order to truly find the blessing in being a good wife. For my fellow single women, you may have learnt from past relationships and experiences what you *don't* want to have in your own marriage. You may also have a heightened false sense of security about what could be received from a man who is simply demonstrating his humanity, and this may disappoint you at one stage and yet bring great joy at another.

God encourages His daughters to ensure they 'have no other god [idol]' (Exodus 20:3), and to ensure with all diligence that they 'keep (themselves) from idols' (1 John 5:21). As you journey through your season of singleness, I believe this is a question to reflect on continuously: Have you made an idol of marriage? Relationships? Status? Have you been disillusioned into thinking you are less valuable than a married woman, or not valued enough as a single woman? We must arise out of the dust and shake off the lies that society and even our close peers bombard us with. God wants to be first in your heart – and only the Word of God can reveal the true condition of where you are at.

The Marriage

God has created marriage between a man and a woman and declares it as good. The 'pioneer and perfecter' (Hebrews 12:2 NIV) of a thing knows what it is able to withstand, and how much joy it can bring when it flourishes in its purpose. We are blessed by God to be joined in matrimony to another for His glory, our transformation and joy. Marriage provides a foundation for any community, as it is the pinnacle of the family, and having both a husband and wife functioning in unity in such an intimate way is powerful. God is all-wise in His creation.

As a single woman, who desires to be married one day (if the Lord wills), I have reflected on what I can do in my season of singleness to enrich my character and life with the knowledge God has given me. God has given us everything we need in every season. God's 'grace is sufficient for you, [His] strength is made perfect in weakness' (2 Corinthians 12:9 KJV). Grace is the unmerited favour of God and the empowerment of God for an individual who can only go so far with their natural abilities, gifts, talents and strength in any and every given circumstance. When we are at the end of our tether, the grace of God comes to aid us in such a phenomenal way.

God will grace you in your season of singleness. He will empower you to do all things with His help and His resources — those things you would ideally want a partner to support you with: the children, the goals, the business, the company, the fulfilment... God is 'the God of all grace...' (1 Peter 5:10 KJV). He gives His daughters grace. He gives you grace to live out your singleness with joy and not sadness, with hope and not defeat, with confidence and not timidity. It is a blessing to be single.

I believe 'waiting' is something key to live by. As a single woman, how you choose to wait will determine whether being single is viewed as an 'endurance' season or an enjoyment one. God wants the latter for you. He wants His daughters to 'wait well'. This refers to your conduct and attitude whilst waiting to be married.

A Christian wife will attest to the many waiting seasons she has in marriage; the patience with oneself and one's husband, as you grow together and change over the years, and the forbearing of challenges and storms that require waiting and waiting well, in order to come through the other side a better and wiser woman.

Waiting well is key for a single woman. 'Wait on the Lord: be of good courage, and He shall strengthen thine heart: wait, I say, on the Lord' (Psalm 27:14 KJV). Your pure conduct and attitude forge your character, and this character is what will enable you to withstand the storms of life and responsibilities of being a good wife. I don't subscribe to the notion of 'having it all together' before being married, as we are not perfect and will never arrive at perfection whilst living on earth. However, what you do with your time will surely bring its rewards in many ways once your season changes.

As a single woman, I am purposeful with my time, whether that is resting and lounging or recuperating. I ensure I 'wait well' by being proactive in my relationships with others. I believe by building myself up in the Lord; I am built up in confidence for the right connections. I am a social person and aim to be prayerful at the same time. I enjoy attending the gym, walking for fitness, going out with friends and family, hosting dinner parties and organising visits, attending events of all kinds — for work, property seminars, women's events — and many miscellaneous things that strengthen my blind spots. I encourage my sisters in the faith to wait well by being proactive with their time.

The Self

I believe your status of singleness is good when developed in the most effective way. By 'effective' I mean living in contentment with the season you are in (however long it may be), as your contentment in this area can permeate to every other area of your life: work, family, relationships, friendships and finances, amongst other things. To be content is to be in a state of peaceful happiness or satisfaction. Can you be satisfied in your season and status of being single? Absolutely. How long does that satisfaction last? As long as *you* want it to. What if I have been single for 20 years, can I *still* be satisfied with my life? Absolutely.

Whatever your status, satisfaction and peaceful happiness are ongoing, not a one-time occurrence. If I eat a meal I really enjoy and I feel satisfied with the quality, the smell, the taste and even the presentation, will I not get hungry again the next day, or even a few hours after the meal? Yes. And I will be seeking out something else to satisfy my taste buds.

It is the same principle with being content in your season and with your status. Finding ways to be completely satisfied and at peace with who you are and where you are at is important. You have to be aware that no person or thing — other than God — has the power to completely give you true, pure comfort, peace and satisfaction. People can be additions to this but, because they are human, they will fall short of perfection. Our desires for God — and living the life He has given us to the fullest — have to be greater than the desires for anything else, otherwise we will be discontent and cast down, constantly seeking fulfilment in the wrong places.

I pursue being content with what I have and where I am at and, in turn, this flows through like a river into every other area of my life. I am content with my friendships and do not seek to take more than I give. I am content in my work life because I can count the many ways it is blessing me, and I am being a blessing in the role I have been entrusted with. In finances, I am content with what I have. Yes, goals and targets are in place, but ultimately, having a large sum of money in the bank does not change my surname any more than if it were a small amount. It isn't what I have that determines my joy, but rather who I am and how I can live. We should be aiming to live with this motto and constantly learning from it: 'In whatsoever state I am, therewith to be content' (Philippians 4:11 KJV). 'You're blessed when you're content with just who you are – no more, no less. That's the moment you find yourselves proud owners of everything that can't be bought' (Matthew 5:5 MSG).

You are blessed because of who you are and not where you are in life. What I mean by this is, you were created *with* a purpose and *for* a purpose. Your life has meaning and value. The value of your life is not dependent upon what stage you are at or what you have, nor whether you are married or whether you 'have it all together' by society's standards. 'Let each person lead the life that the Lord has assigned to him, and to which God has called him…' (1 Corinthians 7:17 ESV). God has assigned life to you; your life doesn't become worth living only once you are married, it is for living *now*!

I want to encourage those who are plundering through the season of singleness, often feeling high and then extremely low in emotion and spirit, because your desire hasn't yet come to fruition. God has not forgotten you. When you feel like you have been forgotten by God, through your many unanswered prayers, tears, conversations, relationships and other challenges, I want to remind you, you are always in His thoughts, and you are precious to Him. 'Every single moment You are thinking of me! How precious and wonderful to consider that You cherish me constantly in Your every thought! O God, Your desires toward me are more than the grains of sand on every shore! When I awake each morning, You're still with me' (Psalm 139:17-18 TPT).

There is no human being in this world who will ever be consumed with loving you and thinking about you the way God your heavenly Father does. He has the best for His daughters and sons, and He is familiar with their ways. He will never lead you to harmful situations without His grace to walk through it and power to overcome.

You have to be resilient to the negative thoughts, feelings and voices all around you. Whatever you give your ear and eye to has great influence over you. God knew we would live in a world filled with many idols and influences. He knew the internal and external pressures we would face. He provided a way for us to live abundantly in Him and through Him in all that comes our way. Whilst our society encourages relationships as a goal of life at any cost (including that which damages your mind, soul and spirit), God is concerned about *you* **at any cost,** and the Lord is constantly interceding for your mind, soul and spirit to be at peace and for all to go well with you.

So, to all the beautiful women out there — especially my beautiful single women — my prayer for you is that you would confidently walk in the life and season God has given you for His glory. I pray that God will give you grace and peace for your journey, and that you will continue to trust in the arms of an unfailing, unchanging and unwavering God, who loves you deeply. May you know that you are not less than another woman who is married, and that your challenges are neither unseen nor unheard of by your Creator - He knows you and cares for you. Live your life with great expectations and pursuits and always, *always*, be prayerful.

With love
Ganel Simms
A fellow single woman

INFORMATION ABOUT THE WRITER

Ganel Simms is by profession a qualified paralegal specialising in private client law. She is currently a national business manager in the Ministry of Justice. She has been a Christian for over 13 years and lives in Birmingham. Ganel is passionate about her faith and is a speaker and teacher of the Word of God.

Connect with Ganel at www.facebook.com/ganel.simms

Email: ganel.simms@gmail.com

SINGLENESS: A TIME FOR UNDIVIDED DEVOTION TO GOD

by Joan B St Louis

'...An unmarried woman or virgin is concerned about the Lord's affairs: her aim is to be devoted to the Lord in both body and spirit. But a married woman is concerned about the affairs of this world – how she can please her husband. I'm saying this for your own good, not to restrict you, but that you may live in a right way in undivided devotion to the Lord' (1 Corinthians 7:34-35, NIV).

In setting out to write this article, I am thinking that the content may cause some people to be extremely unhappy. However, the reality of life and particularly a life of singleness — though not ideal for some — may be the most profitable, that is, from God's point of view.

Being single, having never been married, I couldn't distrust my life, but simply resolve to trust God in what I thought would be just for a season! As difficult as it seemed, this was the time to model a kind of resolution to demonstrate Christlikeness with undivided devotion. Was it easy? No, no and a hundred times no! However, it gave me a keen sense in understanding how powerful our minds are, and how they can work against us!

I never imagined I would or could admit that a life of singleness appears to have been profitable for me. I never imagined that by a certain age I wouldn't be married — with or without children.

At weddings, someone somewhere, including my Pastor, would always find a way to whisper in my ears: "I wonder who's next?" and, for some unknown reason, I would hear myself saying through a smile: "Not me!"

As much as there was the desire to be married one day, I have to admit I never felt under any pressure, but simply believed it would happen for me some day. I believed marriage for me would be in God's own time and, as I got older, accepted that it wasn't my season; the thought that this could last for a lifetime never even crossed my mind!

Like many single people nowadays — and single women in particular — I cannot recall ever wrestling with the thought or knowledge of the possibility I would never be married, or that perhaps God wanted me to remain single! Additionally, I cannot really explain it, but I don't remember ever thinking of how to cope with or handle the emotional stress that can accompany a strong desire for human relationship or companionship. Now I have some understanding of this, which came about during some research for my book, *Created for God's Pleasure: A Challenge for Single Women,* some years ago.

Being in conversation with a number of women, mainly in church and from a variety of socio-economic backgrounds over the years, alerted me to the fact that many women struggle with the possibility of being single even for a season, never mind a lifetime! Some of these women have great difficulty in accepting their status of being single as a 'gift'. I personally believe that in God's scheme of things singleness could very well be one of the greatest gifts, whether for a season or for a lifetime.

Now I can see and even to some extent understand that being single as surely as being married can be a God-given gift, and what one needs to take into consideration of either status is God's will and purpose for our lives.

Many people find it extremely difficult to let go of their dream, and to allow God to make the arrangements for any partnership concerning their current status and indeed their future.

Surrendering my life to Jesus Christ and being in church seemed to have fulfilled a huge part of my time and life. The leadership of my church identified something in me I honestly wasn't even aware of, and with that I was put to work!

Over the past 40 plus years, I have worked through most of the departments or auxiliaries of the church — from Children and Youth Ministries, Sunday School teaching, Hospitality, Women's Ministry, Choir and then Missions and Evangelism… Finally, in this latter department/auxiliary, I can honestly say I've found my niche! It seemed that this was where I belonged, and this should not have come as any surprise to me because I have always loved travelling. In fact, one of the few prophecies spoken over me concerning my life (and ministry) was that "God would have me travel in the ministry"!

Geography, both human and natural, was one of my favourite subjects, having always been fascinated with different places, cultures and languages and, of course, my love for travel. My passion was always in the outdoors, away from the norm, being somewhere different.

How life happened for me is inexplicable. Working full-time in a secular job, and busy with a full church programme, I couldn't say when it dawned on me that years seemed to have gone by when I suddenly realised that my life was full; I was busy *every* day!

Most of my vacations were spent travelling and ministering — nationally to churches, women's groups, evangelism and conferences, and internationally, where I attended conferences, seminars, conventions and went on missions. These activities took me to places I'd never dreamed of, such as Nigeria, South Africa, several states in the US, French Guiana, South America, Haiti, France, Spain, Dominica and Grenada, my birthplace.

I realised these activities seemed to have somehow sneaked up on me, and I had to conclude: "Lord, I am so busy!"

One of the things that has dawned on me is that the desire for a marriage relationship never really goes away. I am discovering, however, that God has so filled my life with what I believe to be His ultimate purpose for me that I have now more or less resigned myself to the fact that singleness for me is not only for a season but possibly for a lifetime.

Speaking now from that perspective, and as someone who has been overtaken by the realisation that God wants me exclusively for Himself, I am left with little or no option but to totally surrender to the Heart of Heaven.

If my dreams, hopes, longings and aspirations are not on the same page as God's will for me, if they are not aligned to His ultimate purpose for me, I am very aware that I will find myself unnecessarily stressed out, so I simply have to succumb to Him and, in the process, save myself from self-inflicted frustrations, borne of trying to reach for something beyond my grasp.

I now believe that totally surrendering myself to God's divine will, calling and purpose for my life means I may have also unwittingly surrendered my rights to individual choices and preferences, such as having someone else in my life who might be a distraction.

For some strange and unknown reason, I believe that my life at this moment in time is being fulfilled simply by serving God, His Church and His people.

I am also very conscious of the Word of God, which says that a person is to be given in marriage. One shouldn't surrender to the temptation to simply take or help oneself to a marital relationship which God has not specifically designed and where devotions can be divided. This thinking could be controversial but is a reality for many people — some of whom may have chosen or helped themselves prematurely. God will not follow or take second place to anyone!

At this moment in time, I do not feel I am missing out by not having a husband, because I think there are many deterrents surrounding present-day marriages, and specifically amongst Christians.

It is sad to admit, perhaps, that I do not find human nature to be trustworthy. In fact, I don't trust anything on two legs!

Apart from this little personal aside, I have to confess I wouldn't consciously pursue marriage at this time of my life.

Present-day society is being ravished by the breakdown of marriages and family life. I guess we can't fathom the depth of sadness for those enduring unhappy marriages or relationships because of the pretense and deception that accompany the discord in some relationships. Everyone is "blessed and highly favoured" in church, but are living on a battlefield at home!

I believe that travelling on a road with someone who isn't keeping to the same lane can create much chaos; for example, a mature single woman, being with someone who may not be on the same spiritual wavelength. As we get older, everything starts to slow down, and it seems that everywhere we turn, our society is plagued with people who are mentally challenged. Sadder still is the fact that the Church isn't exempt from many of these realities and experiences, and this makes the reality of being single a little more attractive.

One of my favourite Bible characters is King David. Yes, I know, not a good representative of singleness, but principally, it was his relationship with God. David spoke to God about almost every decision he was making. We constantly read in the Scriptures: '... and David enquired of the Lord.'

So, using David as an example, I talk to God about almost everything. On a few occasions when I saw or met someone who 'drew my attention', I used to always talk to God or ask whether this was the one or "Should I pursue?" And, quite honestly, the answer was always "No"! However, with the "No", God would always show me something in or about the person that He knows I wouldn't like or want to live with! It may have been something in their mannerisms, attitudes or certain behavioural patterns, so with these signs, I would humbly bow out.

The realisation that Heaven wants me — that the face of God, in all its glory and majesty is turned towards me — is truly overwhelming. This reality then leads me to a place of awe and wonder that the Heavenly Pursuer wants my heart.

As a single Christian woman, I believe I occupy a prominent place in God's plan for His people, His Church and His Kingdom. Thinking reflectively, and with a true desire for God's will, there must be the conclusion that God's timing and purpose must take precedence over any personal aspirations I may have.

I am at a place where I can sincerely confess I have accepted the status of being single with grace and without lamentation, sadness or disappointment. Others may see singleness as an unacceptable plight, albeit one ordained by a loving God and Father who knows what is best for His children.

One thing I believe every single Christian should come to understand is that, having created us and gifted us with His salvation, God reserves the right to keep us to Himself by not giving us away in marriage. He has chosen us for a particular plan and purpose, so that we can serve Him with undivided devotion and without distractions.

Of the many choices we have in life, choosing to serve our Lord Jesus must come first. I have made the choice that God will come first in everything concerning my life. Having brought me through this unprecedented time of a pandemic and lockdowns, there is still this excitement within my heart. Excitement, because I can see the national and international doors God has opened that are just waiting for me to walk through so I can continue to fulfil His purpose for my life.

God's divine direction and approval are very important to me, as is making the right choices. My life in God's hands means I am at the right place and bearing a wonderful testimony of His marvellous grace.

INFORMATION ABOUT THE WRITER

Joan B St Louis is President of the Department of Missions for the Calvary Church of God in Christ, UK. She works locally and nationally with the church to promote missions, evangelism and church growth. She is also involved in assisting the church in France along with a team of like-minded individuals.

Joan travels extensively nationally and internationally to promote the work of the Church. Her main areas of ministry are Bible teaching, intercessory prayer and hospitality, as well as being a conference speaker. Joan is the author of *Created for God's Pleasure: A Challenge for Single Women*. Her ministry on singleness started several years ago, and has been conducted nationally and internationally - mainly to women's groups from Pentecostal/Evangelical backgrounds.

Joan has a diploma in Theology and a BSc (Hons) in Social and Natural Science.

Connect with Joan at www.facebook.com/joan.stlouis.7

Email: joanbstlouis@hotmail.com

TRANSFORMING LIVES AND INITIATING RELATIONSHIPS THROUGH SINGLES' MINISTRY

by Joy Adams

My name is Joy Adams — a member of Cathedral of Praise in Wood Green, London — and I have been a Single Adult Ministry (SAM) co-ordinator for many years.

I love what I do, and I have been blessed to see the lives of single adults healed, delivered, restored, turned around and become on fire in serving God.

I have seen lives transformed and relationships blossom from friendships into marriages.

I have seen singles mobilised and working together on the mission field.

I have seen God use our singles' ministry to inspire others to start their own singles' ministries and awaken individuals to His plan for their lives as single adults and, in the process, find fulfilment in God.

I have also been there to encourage those who have found themselves single again through divorce or widowhood and have offered support to single parents.

I have loved collaborating with other ministers to meet the needs of singles and provide enriching programmes, and I love having 'casual' God conversations which have prompted individuals to make positive changes in their lives. What a privilege to serve God's people in this way.

My Church

I am a member of prominent church denomination, New Testament Church of God (NTCG) UK, founded in 1953 by members of the Windrush generation under the leadership of Dr Oliver A Lyseight.

NTCG is part of the Church of God — a worldwide denomination with branches in 178 countries, a membership of 7 million and whose headquarters are in Cleveland, Tennessee in the US.

Single Adult Ministry (SAM) was started in NTCG UK in 1996, and Wood Green NTCG became one of the first congregations to successfully establish a singles' ministry within the denomination. It was also one of the few singles' ministries in Britain's Black Pentecostal Church at that time. I subsequently joined the National SAM Board, led by Rev David King, and since then we have ministered to thousands of singles. We now also offer support and training to new coordinators who want to start singles' ministries in their own churches.

The Call

I cannot believe that 23 years after I was handed an information pack on the singles' ministry from my church sister, Jacqui, that I am *still* a part of this ministry!

Christ wanted to use my whole life to lead and serve this ministry, so it wasn't something I could just walk away from. I have lived with a sense of purpose and have submitted to God's plan for my life.

When I started the singles' ministry at Cathedral of Praise, I was filled with passion, along with my yet-to-be-harnessed gifts of teaching and exhortation; a love for God's Word; a desire for my relationship with God to remain my priority, and I loved bringing people together. Plus, I had my testimony (which I'll share later).

I discussed the information I'd received about SAM with fellow church member, Brenda, who was involved in the new converts' ministry. She came on board. Looking back, I was a budding new Christian at the time, so Brenda must have thought, 'Let me help this woman.' We were also blessed with a team of enthusiastic singles to kickstart the ministry.

Everyone was excited about SAM Wood Green and the opportunities this ministry offered for singles to socialise, network, fellowship and grow in Christ. Since the very start, we have remained tight ministry buddies, and God has used us to host some phenomenal ministry initiatives to singles within our congregation as well as the wider church community — from youth to seniors. We have also been supported by those who are married, by those who see the value of the ministry. Relationship building lies at the heart of SAM, and this has had a unifying impact on our church.

The Challenges

SAM faced many challenges over the years, which at times came from leadership, from singles, from people's perceptions that SAM was only for those who wanted to get married, from negative stereotypes, stigma and outdated church culture.

I have heard it said: "Why don't you change the name? Why do you have to use the word 'single'?" As individuals we must challenge stigma, otherwise we will rush into marriage out of sheer desperation, like the women found in Isaiah 4:1. The opinions of others shouldn't cause anyone to feel uncomfortable, ashamed or incomplete because they are single. Instead, single Christians should seek a biblical understanding of how God views and uses the single adult and be encouraged to be outstanding individuals who others will admire.

Changing views in society had an impact on ministry. Even the fact that single adults can be transient meant we often had to almost start over and realign with the current group of singles.

Brenda and I faced challenges when working as a ministry team, and there were times when neither of us could agree. It would be either the timing wasn't right, or I couldn't see what Brenda saw and vice versa. Sometimes I felt as though I wasn't even expressing what I believe God had placed inside of me.

I thank God for godly counsellors — my former pastor Bishop Eric and his wife Sis Brown, and my sister friends Lynette, Jen and Brenda, who have been there to support me.

Thanks also to my awesome Dad, Linton, for his consistent prayers, words of wisdom and for always encouraging the ministry God has placed inside of me. There have been some frustrating seasons in ministry, but the Holy Spirit would always come with a reassuring word in due season, and the flame to serve would be reignited again.

We always heard the cry: "Joy and Brenda, when's the next event?" But not only that, there was so much fruit in the lives of those we ministered to that gave testament to what God had done through SAM that we *had* to keep going.

The Ministry

Singles' Ministry at Wood Green has always aimed to empower the single adults we serve. Our ministry events draw individuals closer to God, build stronger relationships and result in spiritual growth. We always provide opportunities for singles to minister. And we know how to have fun.

The mandate God gave me very early on was that people wanted relationships, but they were not healed. God took me personally on a journey of healing to *real-ationship*.

We have to be *real* about the state of our current internal condition and compare it to how God intends it to be. The steps on my journey were: Healing, Deliverance, Restoration, Ministry and Real-ationship, and I would share my experience when speaking at seminars and conferences. I also engaged in targeted intercessory prayer.

Once we allow God to take us through these stages, we will flourish in our relationships and our marriages will last, have purpose, and bring God glory. God was highlighting the importance of our internal condition as a foundation for lasting relationship.

Changes in Society and the Church

Over time, societal attitudes have changed towards singleness, marriage and how people approach relationships. This has meant that individuals remain single for longer, start families later, are willing to raise children alone, co-habit, and use online dating sites to find love. Divorce is also on the rise.

The Church is impacted by these changes in society, with over 45% of the UK population being unmarried and family structures becoming more complex. So, what does this mean for the Church and to the single adults it serves today?

The Church cannot provide spiritual support alone. Leadership must understand the challenges and be aware of the multi-faceted needs of single and single-again adults; provide adequate, relevant teaching and guidance, and also practical and relational support that empowers single adults as they navigate through life. Leadership teams should include married and single people, so that the team contains a range of perspectives and recognises the opportunity to reach unsaved single adults.

Where are all the men?

One reality we have had to face over time is the increasing number of involuntary singleness we see in our Black Pentecostal churches. Single women outnumber single men, which means many women who desire to be married cannot see any marriage prospects within their existing congregations or church circles.

What I observed in this situation was two-fold: women wanted to meet their husbands, but also — more importantly — men needed to be saved.

In our attempts to meet Mr Right we brushed past and overlooked Mr Unsaved or Mr 'He's-Just-My-Brother' or 'Just-My-Friend' and failed to pray for the salvation of men who are already in our lives, such as our children's fathers, our brothers, uncles, cousins, fathers, grandads, friends, etc. When a man gets saved, it can lead to a whole household or friendship group being saved.

I came across a book entitled '*How Women Help Men Find God*' and that was it, I was on a mission. God can use women to bring men into His kingdom. I spoke to men, leaders of men's ministries and to pastors for input on the needs of men, why men did not attend church or, if they did, why they did not stay for long.

After much discussion and collaborating with Brenda and Garnet, who was head of Wood Green NTCG Men's Ministry, we launched 'Prayer Changes Things' — a strategic prayer initiative.

The congregation was mobilised to pray for the salvation of men and for marriages. We ran this series of prayer twice: the first time for eight weeks and then two years later, in 2015, when it ran for almost six months, as the Lord revealed the depths of the issues we had been called to pray into.

Many engaged with this prayer initiative.

We had many visitors to our church and even the chaplaincy at Pentonville Prison joined in the prayers for men to be saved.

These periods of focused prayer for men were effective. Men were delivered, set free and saved. Unsaved spouses came to Christ and marriages were healed. At least seven marriages came out of this time of prayer. People shared testimonies that they met their spouse after attending Prayer Changes Things. One man told me: "Joy, I was struggling with a lot of things, but Prayer Changes Things freed me and shortly afterwards I met my wife. Glory to God!"

Spiritual MOT Weekend Retreats

Spiritual MOT Weekend Retreats are another initiative hosted by SAM.

These weekends give individuals the opportunity to experience quality time out with God, away from the busyness of life. The Holy Spirit gives each person a spiritual check-up which leads to life transformation.

Many lasting friendships have been established at these retreats, and delegates have left with a sense of purpose and clarity on their next steps.

Nadine, one of the delegates, commented: "The MOT helped me to stop grieving for my Mum who had died 17 years ago." God showed her the beauty of His creation in the beautiful surroundings, and she heard God say: "It's enough!"

The time away also helped Nadine to hear God's voice more clearly. She explained: "I didn't believe I could do what God had called me to do. I was fearful, shy and anxious. With the help of the leaders and organisers of MOT, I was able to cement a deeper relationship with God. I was mobilised and ready for ministry!"

Marsha is another person who found attending our Spiritual MOT retreats transformational. She also met her husband on the retreat. She said: "We both started our journey to great friendship from the Spiritual MOT. This event shaped our future to eventually getting married."

And it isn't just women who attend the retreats either. Abraham is one of the guys who attends our retreats regularly. He said: "MOT has provided a regular getaway and opportunity to rejuvenate spiritually with God. It has been one of the most instrumental events in the calendar year for me and for those who experienced it. In addition, SAM led a mission to Grenada, which impacted my friends and me significantly. To try to articulate the impact of every event would be too difficult."

Singleness and Me

For most of my teens and young adult life I chose to follow the crowd and delight myself in parties, clubs and wine bars. As an unsaved young person, having boyfriends and casual relationships was the norm for my friends and me. As far as I was concerned I was having fun. Once I gave my life to Christ, however, I discovered that those apparently harmless relationships had had an adverse effect on my self-esteem and feelings of self-worth.

I had unknowingly caused damage to my soul. I hadn't valued myself and was ignorant to the fact that I had formed spiritual soul ties, which would later need to be broken off my life if I were to be made whole and understand who I was created to be in Christ. Having mistaken sex for love, God had to teach me the true meaning of love and just how much He loved me. I took a lot of convincing.

To get through to me, God used the story of Hosea, the prophet who God told to marry Gomer, a prostitute. Despite her infidelities throughout their marriage, Hosea loved Gomer, and this story serves as a metaphor for God's love for Israel. God also used the story to restore my life and identity.

What a journey of deliverance I have been on! I had been tied to past relationships even though I was single. I thank God I am now whole and free, no longer connected to my past. "If the Son sets you free, you will be free indeed!" (John 8:36)

There are many aspects of my life's journey that God has used to help me minister to single adults on their own. I sincerely want to see singles healed from past relationships and overcome the battles of the mind so they can understand their true identity and walk in their purpose.

I want as many singles as possible to 'Love God's Way': to enter marriages and relationships that glorify God. If sharing my testimony helps, I will continue to share.

Conclusion

As a singles' minister, you have to manage expectations and can only reach those who choose to take part in ministry activities.

I accept that singles' ministry is not for everyone, however each church must ensure they meet the needs and address the issues of its single and single-again congregation from both a biblical and singles' perspective. I have been blessed to partner with God as He transforms people's lives.

The overall vision God has given me for single adults is to empower individuals to serve, so they are made whole and experience relationships — and ultimately marriages — that glorify Him! It's also important to enable single adults to reach a place of contentment in God should they marry or not.

My message to singles is this: if marriage is your heart's desire, do not allow your faith to waiver. You need to take responsibility, prepare yourself with the right resources and be 'Relationship-Ready'! God brings people together in many different ways, so be open to varied opportunities to meet new people.

The ideal person for you could even be known by your close contacts already. Pray and move by faith. Be intentional and take action.

And ladies, please don't just sit there and wait to be found! You have a part to play too. Faith without works is dead!

INFORMATION ABOUT THE WRITER

Joy Adams is an ACCA-qualified accountant who works within the NHS. She has served as a Single Adults Minister for over 20 years and has hosted conferences, seminars and retreats for singles and young adults. Her passion is to empower individuals to fulfil their purpose in Christ through the ministry of intercessory prayer, teaching and exhortation. Joy also has a heart for missions and prison ministry and a desire is to see individuals restored through the love and power of God.

Connect with Joy at www.facebook.com/SpiritualMOT

Email: joyadamsbooks@gmail.com

CAN YOU MAKE JOLLOF RICE?

by Ola Nubi

"Can you make jollof rice?" This was one of the questions I was asked on a date one evening, along with how old I was, why I didn't speak more of my mother tongue, and then a further comment came to mind.

"I'm kind of worried about marriage and all that long-term stuff. I haven't even been in a church longer than two years max, and you are asking me about marriage." Then he laughed.

I tried to laugh as well – a pretend sad kind of laugh because, despite his lack of consistency, I really did like the chap.

Looking back (again), I had the wrong motives. I wanted all my family members to love me and treat me with respect. I wanted to be 'normal' just like them, I guess, instead of being the centrepiece of family discussions as the 'Big Auntie who wasn't married at 40-plus and beyond' — the object of pity, scorn and all the kind of self-help advice on how to solve the issue even though I was a praying Christian. There was always someone who believed they knew someone who could pray 'the perfect prayer' to cure me of my singleness.

How do you live an emotionally healthy life for 30 years of praying, fasting and believing God for something, and it hasn't happened as and when you wanted it to happen? Add family stress and social expectations to the mix, and it all begins to get a bit too much sometimes.

Emotions are on a roller coaster. There would be good days and bad days. On the good days, I am full of the Word and full of faith that God will bring me a husband. On the bad days, however, I wasn't so full of the Word. I didn't feel like praying, and I would be drawn into the rabbit hole of social media and feast my eyes on all the glossy Big Nigerian Weddings on Instagram.

***

Waiting 101
The elective many of us can't wait to get rid of
We keep on waiting because we thought that to do anything else was sinful.
Then one day...
We wake up to the clanging noise of a thousand biological clocks.
The sound reverberates, shattering every iota
Of our self-imposed façade of contentment.

How can you expect to find a husband if you cannot guarantee your husband an heir? OK, hang on. You sound like something from a Jane Austen movie, I hear you say, but these expectations for male children are no joke, along with expectations of fertility, so you can't afford to hang about — especially if you are planning on having a Big Great Nigerian Wedding, which is part of the Nigerian Dream we grow up to believe we are entitled to.

It's always there at the back of your mind.

Nollywood expectations

I went through school, like so many others in Nigeria, believing that 'The One' would magically metamorphose somewhere between matriculation and graduation. This is something you are prepared for and have prayed through from the time you learn how to hold a broom. This is a country where the ultimate insult is to point at a woman who has annoyed you and utter, "You will never marry", for not to marry is a case for shame – for yourself and your family. To not marry is to be pitied. To be thought of as being cursed. To be seen as someone who has come into the world to achieve nothing. A prayer uttered for single women by their mothers and aunties is 'O *ni waiye ason*'.

Basically, you are a failure.

Being a Christian doesn't really change how you are seen in that community. The annual prayer line for singles is mostly women, with the single men trying their best to fade into the background, beset with their own battles that sometimes render them unable or unwilling to commit.

At social gatherings people will give you 'the look', or hold on more tightly to their husbands, or start talking over your head about their children who are graduating or getting married, and you just learn over the years to perfect your poker face. One will be thought of as carnal and worldly to still want to be married — especially when one has reached the mature age of 40-plus. Why not just accept your lot and become a 'senior church auntie'?

Self-worth and validation in Christ and Christ alone

No matter how strong you are emotionally, sometimes you are made to feel like you are less than by friends or family members, and sometimes it's more internal; you are struggling with your own feelings of self-worth — especially in a culture where marriage is seen as a woman's purpose in life, and attainment is seen as the pinnacle of life's ambition. In short, if you are single, you have missed the mark in the eyes of many and, in some cases, they will actually tell you that to your face — just so you are aware of your colossal failure to live up to their expectation of being the Perfect Nigerian Daughter.

The Nigerian organisational chart of social standing

Just where does a mature 40-plus single woman fit into the social network system in churches, which are mostly heavily family-orientated? Sometimes family gatherings, like weddings, funerals or Christmas holidays, tend to exacerbate the feelings of 'otherness' or not quite fitting in with the norm.

You see, there is this thing I call the 'Nigerian organisational chart'. It's an unwritten code. At top of the chart are the 'married with boys', followed by the 'married with boys and girls', then comes the 'married with girls', 'divorced with children', 'single parents', 'married without children', 'divorced without children' and, at the bottom - the lowest common denominator — are those 'single women', who have never married or had a child. For these folk, no professional or financial attainment, church title or award can ever move them up the ladder. Only a husband or having a child can do that.

If you, as a single person, ever forget where you are in that organisational chart, there will always be a look, a snide comment, or something to remind you just where your marital status has placed you.

This is what sometimes causes the low self-esteem. It messes with your inner peace and security, and makes you socially withdrawn, feel unloved and unwelcome — both in your community and church — and the measure of your worth is seen only in what you contribute to the running of the church.

Church has the role through its leadership (pastors, in particular) to assist and help the damaged image and self-esteem that singles might feel in their respective communities and churches. It is important that a church programme delivers structured care and counselling, in order to minister to people who are separated, divorced, widowed or never married.

To be single is to be seen as someone who has a 'problem'.

I have learnt over the years to realise that I *don't* have a problem, because I know where my validation and true value come from; they come from God. He has loved me into wholeness, so that when I come up against mindsets that try to define me or put me down due to my marital status, it doesn't detract from my self-identity or value.

I am loved.

I am special.

He has healed, blessed and redeemed me.

He has given me a task and a calling to fulfil that no one on the face of this earth can do the way I do.

In the years of waiting, the enemy will take several shots at your faith, your armour and your confidence, by using others to dent any self-confidence that being single for several years hasn't already eroded.

Some of us find ourselves approaching another single decade: 30, 40…. or 50. Many may smile or pretend it doesn't hurt, but I will put my hand up and admit: sometimes it *does* get you down.

Many of us have spent most of our lives focused on the Lord, ministry and education, building relationships with family, friends and career. Without a husband or children, it was easy to occupy ourselves doing things we felt God was leading us to do and, when we were younger, it was OK. Not perfect but it was OK.

Then the years passed, and you had to deal with the questions being thrown at you by well-meaning and sometimes not-so-well-meaning acquaintances and family members: "What is going on?" You were asking yourself the exact same questions, only they thought you were being choosy. You were dealing with the same fears as to whether you could have a full, interesting, godly life without a husband. Everyone who seemed to be preaching the 'be content as a single' sermon is married! I've even seen the kids I taught in Sunday school marry and have children and look at me with varying levels of perplexity.

Depression

Depression is the 'elephant in the room' — usually ignored or something to be 'cast out' of you. Something that — if you pray long enough — will disappear. Sometimes it doesn't. Sometimes it stays around, if it's connected to (for example) believing God for a relationship that will lead to marriage, or if you are secretly mourning for the family of your own that you feel has eluded you.

Coming through the valley of longing, desperation can be a wilderness experience. The Israelites spent 40 years in theirs. Ours depends on our willingness to find out from God what His plans and purposes are in the midst of our individual wilderness experiences.

A quiet acceptance

While I'm single, Lord, show me the purposes and plans You have for me.

While I'm single, Lord, show me what You want me to do with the experiences I have faced, the pain of what I've been through, the things people have said to me, the things I have said to myself.

He will use it for His glory. He will use us to encourage and cheer someone else who is walking through their own wilderness. Maybe the same comfort and inspiration you received during your own dark moment is what you can give to others.

I started looking at my life, and what I could do to fulfil my destiny where I was, with the gifts and calling God had given me. Today. Right now. Single. Sometimes worried about my future. Wondering about Bae. Would we ever find ourselves? Would people ever stop asking me where he was? I wasn't sure whether I was meant to go find him or keep waiting for him to find me. I had read so many books from Elisabeth Elliott's *Passion and Purity*, to Michelle McKinney Hammond's books on singleness. I had a whole library of books on singleness, and a couple on marriage.

Some of the books said 'Pray and wait', while some of them advocated the more hands-on approach: go out and socialise, join a dating club or introduction agency.

I'm here now.

I'm living it.

I had adopted the hermitic approach of fasting and prayer, bringing out the same prayer point for over 20 years. I can bring out all my notebooks with the prayer points, and most of them have been answered.

Yet I wait.

I wait with others. We live in this parallel universe alongside our sistren who are treated with the respect and consideration that comes when you are married and have a family. The congratulations are more effusive. You get the approval of leadership — and possibly promotion to a post — because sometimes it is assumed you are more capable and responsible, because you are part of a family unit.

But I thought we had a family. The family of Christ that is above the Nigerian organisational chart.

I speak that kind of family into being, on behalf of all the mature single women out there — a more supportive and empathetic, effective family network for the involuntarily singles, who, after decades of being single, are no longer content to act like they are content, because we aren't fooling anyone – especially God.

INFORMATION ABOUT THE WRITER

Ola Nubi is an award-winning writer and author of seven books including *Love's Persuasion* and *Lovers, Leavers and Keepers; a Christian romance.*

A speaker, poet and blogger she plans to run creative writing classes for those interested in taking their desire to write further in the future.

Ola is passionate about seeing people achieve their potential and enhance their emotional resilience and intelligence and is currently working on a book for mature Christian singles. Her current historical fiction manuscript, highlighting the Black British experience post WW2, has secured a traditional publisher.

You can connect with Ola at www.olanubi.com and @olaawonubi on Instagram.

Email: busywrites@gmail.com

WHEN, GOD, WHEN?

by Andrea Best

From as far back as I can remember, I had always gone to church, so technically that environment was the only one I knew. This was instrumental to how I grew up, eventually shaping who I was to become.

I attended a Pentecostal church — the Church of God of Prophecy — with my parents and siblings. It has many branches across the country and worldwide, and I went to a branch based in North West London.

The membership was predominately made up of individuals from the Black community, who had immigrated from the Caribbean, and it was very much close-knit, and family-oriented in its structure.

My time growing up as a young person in the church was a positive one, and I eventually gave my heart to the Lord around the age of 14.

When I was old enough to be a bit more independent, and had purchased a car to take me here, there and everywhere, I attended various social events, such as concerts, programmes, youth camps and youth conventions. The list was endless. I enjoyed this time of my life, as it kept me occupied and grounded. Also, this period afforded me great opportunities to make lasting and rich friendships, most of which still exist to this day.

Growing up in church, I came to recognise that marriage was an important part of church culture, with the elders modelling what a godly marriage should look like. And, as I came of age, I recall attending many weddings of friends who had connected at the very youth camps and youth conventions we had attended together annually.

At that time, I thought it was exciting to attend and be a part of their weddings. Yet I had this deep desire to be married myself one day, and there was this sense that I wanted it to happen by the age of 19.

I wasn't worried or phased by such a prospect, because in my mind, I had seen friends tie the knot, one after the other. I felt it was a given that I too would make the transition from single to married woman at some juncture.

Well, the age of 19 came and went, but nothing materialised on the marriage front. Yet young people were still connecting with each other, and marriages were flowing in abundance. This wasn't anything out of the ordinary as, by church standards, it was considered a very natural part of life. Therefore, I didn't give it a second thought, whilst waiting for my own time to come. However, the age I wanted to be married at kept increasing — from 19 to 25 and then 30, but still, no joy.

In hindsight, when I reflect over my life growing up in the church, if someone had told me when I was 14, that I would reach my mid-50s, having never been married or birthed a child of my own, I would have thought they were smoking something they shouldn't have been, and would have laughed in their face.

And yet that is my reality today.

As I scrutinise further the state of the weddings I attended in my 20s, the reality is that not all those marriages stood the test of time. Sadly, many ended in divorce. I often wonder whether those couples were even compatible with one another in the first place; or whether they knew the enormity of what they were getting themselves into, and what it actually meant to be a husband or wife.

I believe premarital counselling in the church has only emerged within the last 15 years or so. Had it been around earlier, perhaps some of those marriages might not have gone ahead. And as Christians don't practise sex before marriage, dealing with raging hormones might also have been a stronger incentive for some to get married.

The older I get, the more I am finding that the wait isn't always easy. It has been quite challenging at specific times and milestones in my life. But, with God's help, walking out this season has been possible.

Don't get me wrong. I'm still human and my emotions are very real, and I have had to deal with the internal questions that surface, such as wondering why God chose *me* to embark on this journey, whilst others have been blessed with what I have always longed for and desired.

There are times I have asked God why am I still single and haven't yet met my godly spouse, but He isn't always vocal on the matter. In fact, it feels as though He has remained silent, when all I really want is some reassurance and that crucial answer to the question: Is it a Yes, No or Maybe?

In my late 20s and entering into my 30s, I started to notice there was a definite turn in the tide. Opportunities were becoming few and far between, in terms of men and women meeting each other with a view to marriage. The natural trend I'd seen in my teens was now an entirely different ballgame. The rules had changed, the goalposts had been shifted, and this new 'trend' had crept up on the Church... unchallenged.

I observed how hard things were getting, and made up my mind, quite early on, that if I was to survive and get through this season with my sanity intact, I would have to develop a focused and strong mindset. I didn't want my whole life to be consumed by the idea of whether I was to be married or not, only to get caught up in a cycle of frustration.

God gave me two Scriptures to stand on during this season, which have strengthened and upheld me to this day — like Moses, when his arms were supported by Aaron and Hur at those crucial times when he felt as though they were faltering (Exodus 17:11-12).

'"For I know the plans I have for you," declares the Lord, "plans to prosper you and not to harm you, plans to give you hope and a future"' (Jeremiah 29:11 NIV).

'For the Lord God is a sun and shield; the Lord bestows grace and favour and honour; no good thing will He withhold from those who walk uprightly' (Psalm 84:11 AMP).

Off the back of these two Scriptures, I have lived my life to the full, maximising and embracing this season. I have always loved travelling and have been blessed to visit many amazing countries.

I have also been able to take ministry trips, speaking in countries, such as Jamaica, Spain, the Sudan, Uganda and South Africa, to name but a few. These trips have been enlightening in terms of the individuals I've ministered to; namely, women's conferences and equipping young women in the area of purity. I often found that my own personal purity testimony was something that baffled the young women I encountered and was a hot topic of conversation during Q & A sessions.

These sessions are the highlight of my trips, as I get to impart the knowledge I have learnt growing up as a young Christian, and I effectively get to pass the baton on to the next generation to run their race with dignity and grace.

Again, reflecting over those earlier years, I encountered many women who had adopted the stance of putting their lives 'on hold' whilst waiting for their Boaz to whisk them off their feet. That meant the house was put on hold, as was the car, the holidays and generally just doing life or achieving anything of great significance for themselves.

Even though it would be lovely to experience such milestones with a husband, I decided I couldn't put my life on hold, whilst the years rolled by. This led me to write my book for mature singles, encouraging them to live their lives to the max, whilst glorifying God, regardless of their status. I have managed to stay positive and refuse to allow my single status to define me or cause me to be bitter. I also wanted to encourage others, who were sharing a similar experience to me, not to lose heart as they walk out this journey.

I have to be honest, though, the apparent lack of opportunities for individuals to connect and interact with each other in this day and age is a concern to me. This is so different to what I experienced growing up. It's also the same narrative and concern I hear from single women across the country.

I don't believe there is a shortage of events being organised for individuals to connect, since I have attended a number of these events. I think the frustration is that most of these events are predominately attended by women. I always leave afterwards, having met another new group of girlfriends, and exchanging mobile numbers. And, as much as I like meeting new people, I'd like to have some male friendships too. Sadly, it almost seems as though men are sending out a clear message by choosing to vote with their feet, and not attend events that carry the 'singles' connotation.

I'm not sure why this is the case or what can be done to nurture single men and women to fellowship with each other. But something needs to change, to prevent churches being filled with a number of unfulfilled individuals, who feel their needs are not being met.

I am part of a group in my local church, where we facilitate mature Christian singles to encourage and support one another to navigate this journey. The group consists of beautiful, accomplished godly women, and my heart goes out to them as we meet up monthly, yet there is no change in any of us meeting our future husbands. I often imagine that if I had a man to introduce to each of them, I would gladly step into that role of matchmaker. However, the truth is that I'm just not meeting that core group of single brothers to enable me to do so, which in the 21st century I feel is disconcerting.

Regrettably, there have been some Christian women who have been tired of the wait and, like Sarah in the Bible, have taken matters into their own hands. Whether that is to date and marry an unbeliever, or their biological clock has been ticking too loudly, they went ahead and gave birth to the child (or children) they so desired. Whilst I have never felt I wanted to explore either of those options, I do know what it is like to sit in the seat of the older brother, as in the story of the Prodigal Son.

You will recall in this story the younger brother decided he wanted his inheritance early and left home, squandered all his money, and had to run back home in disgrace. However, his father was so pleased to see him, and was not concerned with the circumstances. Yet, it was another story with the older brother.

'But the elder brother became angry and deeply resentful and was not willing to go in; and his father came out and began pleading with him. But he said to his father: "Look! These many years I have served you, and I have never neglected or disobeyed your command. Yet you have never given me [so much as] a young goat, so that I might celebrate with my friends; but when this [other] son of yours arrived, who has devoured your estate with immoral women, you slaughtered that fattened calf for him!" (Luke 15:28-30, AMP).

I have had to ask God to deal with my heart, whenever I have made comparisons of my life with those who left the church and came back with the child or hubby I had patiently been waiting *in* the church for. There was a misguided sense of entitlement in feeling that God should reward me for the faithfulness I had showed to Him. And whilst He is a just God and rewards faithfulness, the reality is that the only thing promised to me is eternal life. Everything I get to experience in this world aside from that is a bonus.

Hand on heart, even though singleness can be hard at times — especially having waited since I was in my teens — I can honestly say that I am not mad at God, nor have I ever been. Yet, I still feel it is natural to ask God those deep questions, which I often do when I haven't always understood the 'whys' of this life. David also knew what that felt like when he wanted answers from God and cried out: "How long, O Lord? Will You forget me forever? How long will You hide Your face from me? How long must I take counsel in my soul, having sorrow in my heart day after day? How long will my enemy exalt himself and triumph over me? Consider and answer me, O Lord, my God" (Psalm 13:1-3, AMP).

As I continue to wait, I have to believe God is still for marriages and that, in His eyes, they have not gone out of fashion. That is why I remain optimistic that 'he' is still out there, and that it will happen at the God-ordained time.

'Now the Lord God said: "It is not good (beneficial) for the man to be alone; I will make him a helper [one who balances him – a counterpart who is] suitable and complementary for him"' (Genesis 2:18, AMP).

If God hasn't given up on something He has ordained, then neither should God's people. We owe it to ourselves as His Church to seek His face in this matter, and to follow the blueprint He has set out in His Word.

There is a song by Elevation Worship called '*Do It Again*', which sums up how I feel about God as I continue to wait with hope and expectation in this season.

Waiting for change to come,
Knowing the battle's won.
For You have never failed me yet.

Your promise still stands,
Great is Your faithfulness, faithfulness.
I'm still in Your hands,
This is my confidence,

I am encouraged that it is *our* God who moves those seemingly immovable mountains, and He will make a way where there seems to be no way for us, as we navigate this season of our lives.

Yet, in all these things, we are more than conquerors (Romans 8:37).

INFORMATION ABOUT THE WRITER

Andrea Best is the author of two books, *'Insightful Tips for the Unique Mature Single In Her 'Wait' For Mr Right'* and *'Second Glances'*, a romantic novel. Andrea has spoken at several women's conferences in the UK, as well as in Sudan, Uganda and South Africa. She is passionate about seeing young women empowered and walking in their full potential in God, and facilitates a small monthly group for mature singles.

You can connect with Andrea at www.facebook.com/andrea.best.184007

Email: andrea@newlifebible.net

Do It Again lyrics © Worshiptogether.com Songs, Sixsteps Music, Said And Done Music, Markkragenpub, Thank You Music Ltd.

A JOURNEY TO SELF-LOVE

by Jeūanita Swaby

I am a single, young woman, who has been brought up in the Church.

I come from a generation where both sides of my family are heavily involved in church work and ministry. My father is a pastor, and my uncles and aunts are ministers with their own ministries.

I would describe myself as a modern woman who has 'lived a little', with many life experiences, but I realised true fulfilment is to be found in Jesus Christ. I made the decision to give my life to the Lord when I was 14. Looking back, I feel if I hadn't made the decision to follow Him then, I probably wouldn't have done so now.

I remember the day I made the decision to accept Jesus. One Sunday I went to visit my uncle's ministry in Nottingham. After he'd finished preaching, he asked if anybody wanted to be prayed for. I felt led to go to the altar and told my uncle I wanted to be saved. He replied he would pray and ask God to come into my heart. I felt the presence of God and it is a feeling I will never forget. My uncle hugged me and told me he was proud of me. I got baptised and filled with the Holy Spirit later that year. My uncle sadly passed away in 2009, and I still miss him very much.

To be honest, though, I didn't take my faith in God as seriously as I should have. I was young and wanted to be like my non-Christian friends: to do whatever I pleased, and not be known as "the church girl". I enjoyed dressing up, partying and having a good time. I wanted to explore, and I had a lot of questions regarding Christianity. I was a typical teen and had posters of B2K and other rap/RnB artists — cut out from *Young Voices* magazine — covering my wall. I had so many posters on my wall, you could hardly see the wallpaper! Whenever my gran would come and visit, she would jokingly ask: “Jeūanita, how can you sleep with so much popstar on your wall?”

Going to church every Sunday had become the norm, and I got tired of going. I was going to church to please my family, and my faith started to waiver. Mum would always encourage me to go to church and say that even if I just went to church and sat in the presence of God amongst other believers who provided prayer and support, it would be the best place for me to receive a breakthrough.

I eventually stopped going to church for several years but started going again when I was going through a difficult time and needed the prayer and support. Prior to recommitting my life to God, I went through situations that left me feeling weak, fed up, frustrated and alone. I dated men that, on reflection, were not suitable; mixed with people who were no good for me; went through two tough bereavements and indulged in too much retail therapy. I was the modern-day woman at the well. I needed to speak to someone but was fearful of offloading and being judged. I didn’t feel worthy or deserving and found it hard to ask anyone for help — let alone my Saviour Jesus Christ, who knows everything I have ever done.

I had to find God again for myself, understand who He is and learn to trust Him. I needed to find the same zeal I had when I first got saved in my teens. It wasn’t an easy season but, no matter what life threw at me, my mum would constantly remind me of Proverbs 3:5-6. She would always tell me things wouldn’t stay the same but would change with faith and conviction. She stood on that word.

One day, whilst watching YouTube videos, a video of an overseas evangelist came up on my feed. She was sharing her story about her past life and how God had blessed her with a husband. Her story resonated with me, and I reached out to her. We became close and she shared great words of wisdom and helped me to get back on track with my relationship with God and reading the Bible.

One night the evangelist encouraged and prayed for me. When I came off the phone, I heard the phrase ‘Woman at the well’ in my spirit. I wasn’t very familiar with this Bible story but I’d heard it mentioned before.

To understand more about that story and how it related to me, I was led to fast for seven days. Going on the fast, as well as studying Scripture, caused me to look deep within myself and self-reflect. I realised I was lost and needed to find who I was. I also needed to know what God's Word said about me, what my values were, and why I thought and acted the way I did. This was the start of my journey to self-love, self-acceptance and repentance.

Going on the fast caused me to have a dream that spoke deeply about my approach to dating and relationships. In the dream I was on a date, having a good time. I then looked at my phone and noted I had missed calls from another man (with whom I'd had a close relationship) and knew immediately I shouldn't have been on my current date. I felt bad for settling and entertaining someone who wasn't right for me just because I wanted to be in a relationship.

I should have waited for the guy who had called me, but because we were in different seasons, he wasn't ready for me. The timing wasn't right. I kept trying to call him back, but the phone line was dead.

When I woke up from that dream, I realised God was telling me to wait and not settle, to focus on Him and not get distracted. I needed the empty well within me to be filled with His living water and not with a man. Sometimes we know we deserve so much better, but we hold onto what isn't good and only temporary, instead of waiting for something permanent. If I didn't take the time to build a relationship with God, I wouldn't understand His love, what I truly deserve or know my worth.

Undergoing self-reflection and accountability was very necessary for me too. When we make ourselves accountable, we become totally responsible for our actions and mistakes, take ownership, learn, and move on from the experience in a positive way. When we refuse to be accountable, we won't be in the right state of mind to accept in order to heal, learn and change. I had to get to the place where I had to look at myself, the decisions I'd made and their consequences. It wasn't an easy thing to do, but it was about being true to myself.

When I think about where I was and how God has brought me through to where I am now, all I can say is "Thank You, Jesus." God is so faithful. Were it not for His grace and mercy I wouldn't be here today.

There is song by Dorinda Clark-Cole, called '*I'm Still Here*', which has been my anthem and testimony for a while. I can relate to every word. Jesus rescued me and positioned strong women of faith in my life to help me through, which I am so grateful for. God has been with me every step of the way — even though there are times when He would be silent and I would wonder 'God, where are You?' It would be so frustrating at times, but then in His own special way He would show up and let me know He is right there. He is also a healer. I am a living witness that He will mend your broken heart and put you back together again if you allow Him to do so.

I used to be very confident as a teenager up until my 20s, but then trauma and life experiences altered my confidence and how I viewed myself. I had to learn to fall in love with myself again and to let go of toxic people in my life who were causing me more harm than good.

I had to deal with the insecurities that had me bound, and acknowledge my pain and the different ways I would try to fill the void in my life. I needed to let go of all the weight I had been carrying and put my trust in God.

There were times when I would pray: "Jesus, please hug me and let me feel Your presence. Let me know You are here with me and help me to believe You are real. Meet me at my point of need so I can be set free. I no longer want to feel this way; I want to see myself as You see me. This is not who I am." I began to read Scriptures that told me what God thought about me and how He saw me. Afterwards I had canvases made with those Scriptures along with positive I AM affirmations, and displayed them around my room to remind me who I am in Christ Jesus.

We have to allow the Lord to have complete control over our lives and not try to figure things out or try to make things work on our own. When we put our faith and trust in Him, we must give whatever it may be to Him and we leave it with Him. Jesus is Lord and has all power and authority. If we are trusting in Him with all our heart, there is no room for anything (or anyone) else to be in control except Him.

We will never know what happened to the Samaritan woman years later. I wondered if she got married again or if she remained single and continued to share her testimony about her encounter with Jesus at the well with other women in her community. For years she had been looked down on and treated as an outcast, but after her talk with Christ, she had the people of Samaria's full attention, and they believed her report. She now had a *new* reputation and purpose just through that one life-transforming encounter.

Women are constantly being told they should get married. My initial view on life was to get a career, marriage and then children, however I have learnt this is not the case. Our plans and God's plans do not always line up, and whilst marriage is important, we know God wants us to put Him first. Once we put Him first, everything else will fall into place.

There were times when I would be watching a movie or catching up on a sitcom and I couldn't concentrate. That's when I knew I had to pray and spend some time with God and His Word. It's so comforting to pray and dwell in God's presence; it's as though He holds us with a warm embrace and we feel safe to just share everything with Him.

When we meditate on His Word, we get a deeper understanding of it. Whenever we are in a battle, or whenever there is turbulence in our lives, the Holy Spirit will quicken God's Word that is appropriate to our situation. God would always remind me of Jeremiah 29:11. This Scripture follows me everywhere and I just smile because God is reassuring me of His Word.

The single season can be a beautiful thing. It is all about our perspective and what we do during the time to work on becoming a better version of ourselves. That can make all the difference.

Take your focus off how long you are waiting, and truly become occupied with the things of God and enjoy your life. Here are a few things I found helpful and have been doing during my single season:

- Attending women prayer groups
- Therapy
- Listening to podcasts and YouTube influencers who speak about self-love
- Attending online singles' retreats
- Pampering sessions
- Eating healthily and exercising
- Treating myself once a month
- Journalling, spending time in the Word and prayer
- Forgiving others and learning to forgive myself
- Separating from toxic friends
- Saying No and putting myself and my feelings first
- Self-care Saturday
- DIY projects
- Learning a new skill
- Building new relationships and connections
- Helping others
- Being mentored
- Praying for my future spouse
- Trying new things to get out my comfort zone

In my journey I have found joy in serving God and taking the steps to walk in purpose. I have learnt that true and lasting happiness is not ultimately dependent on your relationship status. True happiness is when your heart becomes stable in the Lord.

Were it not for God protecting me, separating me and allowing me to go through past experiences, I would not have blossomed into the woman I am today. I give God all the praise for everything He has brought me out of. He had to strip away the old and prepare my heart and mind to be ready for the new things He has in store for me. God is doing so many wonderful things in my life. It's all coming together like a jigsaw puzzle.

The dream I had has been a constant reminder that true fulfilment is found in Jesus, and I need to wait on Him. I have been using this season to grow as an individual, and focus on my career, my relationship with the Lord and my purpose.

INFORMATION ABOUT THE WRITER

Jeūanita Swaby is a young Christian woman from South London whose faith is the most important thing in her life. Ambitious and determined, Jeūanita is a digital PR executive. She enjoys event planning and has an interest in concert promotion. Jeūanita desires to encourage, empower and support teenage girls and young women to grow in faith and fulfil their potential.

Email: jeuanitaswaby@outlook.com

MARRIED, RE-SINGLED AND MATURE

by Zina Arinze

I remember, as a little girl, how fairy tales were my reference points for falling in love and getting married. It was all about me, the wonderful single princess beautiful, being swept off my feet by my very own prince.

Trust me, I said "I do" in fairy tales *decades* before I ever met the man who became my husband.

In my virtual reality he held me in his strong, loving embrace; our lips entwined, finishing each other's sentences, and eyes locked gazing intently at each other for hours on end, as if time had stood still just for the two of us.

All I ever thought about was that at some stage I would grow up and meet the man of my dreams. He would whisk me off my feet; we'd get married; the church would shout "Amen"; we'd have 2.4 children and live happily ever after. It was the stuff they say dreams are made of and we would not DIVORCE!

I didn't actually know or understand that word.
Divorce was dirty and scandalous.
I grew up believing it was wrong.

Everyone I knew in my close-knit African community in London was married and had kids. I remember an auntie of mine had been married for years but had no kids. She and her husband adopted a son, but no one ever spoke about it – even adoption in the '70s was a silent taboo.

I became a born-again Christian in my teens and didn't ever anticipate not getting married because that was the expectation. Every Nigerian girl got married, full stop. That was the dream and aspiration. Going down this divorce journey was never even at the back of my mind — or anyone else's mind I knew for that matter.

Fast forward to today, in my 50s (just about holding onto them!) and I am single, or some people like to call it *re*-singled. Yes, I did the marriage thing, not the fairy tale I would have liked or imagined; it didn't work out and we got divorced.

Knowing what I know now from the work I have been so privileged to do with married and divorced Christian women, there are soooo many better actresses than I ever was. Some of you may even be reading this now…

Re-Singled and Mature

As a re-singled, mature, divorced Christian woman in the Black Church, the emotions and feelings you go through are excruciating. You are judged and subtly condemned for not being woman enough and wise enough to save your marriage and build your home. 'A wise woman builds her home, but a foolish woman tears it down with her own hands' (Proverbs 14:1 NLT).

For me, the silent, hushed looks and the holding onto husbands even more tightly whenever I was in the vicinity have been incredibly hurtful and sad.

It didn't matter what the backstory was, you were expected to stay married and, trust me, I tried to. I didn't have the courage to initiate divorce proceedings. What would people say about me? Also, as a Christian, I didn't want the guilt of being the one pressing for divorce on my conscience. Even when the papers were served on me, based on two years with consent, I refused to sign them. Five years later, he didn't need my consent and got the divorce anyway. Now, in hindsight, I can say I wasted years by not signing those papers.

The truth of the matter was that my marriage was bad, but I was in denial. I went from one church night vigil to another, interceding for my marriage. I would wake up at midnight, praying to God with my husband's photo as a point of contact for God to restore us and for my husband to love me. I also devoured every single Christian book on marriage and family life I could find. Stormie Omartian's

The Power of a Praying Wife was my go-to resource. Still, we were where we were, and the marriage ended. The learning point for me and for everyone reading this: it takes two to make, work at and save a marriage.

I didn't understand this at the time because I was drowning in shame. I felt deeply guilty at being unable to save my marriage, and believed I had failed God, failed my daughters, my family and the entire body of Christ worldwide. The sheer magnitude of my inner emotional turmoil and spiritual guilt was devastatingly unbearable. I thought I would lose my mind, but grace kept me.

I also recall being newly divorced at events like family reunions and family conventions in my church. I would keep my wedding ring on because I couldn't deal with the condemnatory glances or the questions: "Where is your husband?" or "How is your husband?" I loved the idea of being married, of being a wife and, even though it was evident my marriage was sinking sand, I was focused at staying married at all costs.

If you are reading this, my advice is that if you have a friend or a church member going through marriage issues or a divorce, please don't condemn him or her — especially her — and make it worse. It's a very lonely place to be in; she needs your encouragement and support even if you don't understand or agree with the whys and wherefores. When dealing with her, if you don't have anything helpful to say, just *listen*.

Today, healed, with a healthy re-establishment of my identity in Christ, I have found being re-singled as a woman of God in the extended African church setting to be quite a unique and precarious position to be in, especially as this was coupled with becoming a single mother too.

The general view is, firstly, you dared to get divorced; then secondly, you did so without any regard for your children; thirdly, without considering the negative statistics associated with single motherhood, and fourthly, oblivious to the so-called defined outcome for children raised by single mothers, you go and throw your faith and opinions of others to the wind and become a single mother.

So now I am divorced and a single, mature mother.

It's fair to say that for the divorced, single mother, the blended family is a reality for many homes in today's church and is still unchartered waters for a host of pastors and ministries. My advice is, rather than trying to do this based on your flesh or personal views or ideologies, the Bible — our blueprint — is ever available to help. It says in James 1:5 (NIV): 'If any of you lacks wisdom, you should ask God, who gives generously to all without finding fault, and it will be given to you.'

The Bible is full of Scriptures about remarriage and adultery, and I know many a divorced, Christian woman wanting to remarry has read them all. I know *I* have. The Bible also makes a lot of positive, sympathetic references to widows with and without children. The Black Church today has followed suit: very sympathetic and filled with compassion for *widowed*, single mothers, whereas *divorced*, single mothers are not looked upon as favourably.

I can count how many times I have been asked to contribute towards supporting a widowed, single mother, but I don't recall *ever* being asked to contribute to support a divorced, single mother or even ever receiving that support on my own journey.

I guess the misunderstanding of one of the most contended and difficult verses in the Bible — namely, Malachi 2:16 which says: '"For I hate divorce!" says the Lord, the God of Israel. "To divorce your wife is to overwhelm her with cruelty," says the Lord of Heaven's Armies. "So, guard your heart; do not be unfaithful to your wife"' — could be attributed as the reason for the lack of compassion in the Church towards divorced, single mothers. And, I find, in divorce situations, Christian women are vilified, and divorced men are not.

The Bible is rather non-committal about single motherhood specifically, although divine inference can, of course, be taken from the story of Naomi, the single mother of the newly bereaved family and with Ruth, her daughter-in-law. Again, we have the story in Genesis of Hagar, Sarah's Egyptian maid, who was put out with her son to wander in the wilderness. Hagar had given birth to

Abraham's first son but, due to Sarah's jealously, was made to leave her home.

And then there's the story of Tamar in Genesis 38, who became a single mother by giving birth to twins after sleeping with her father-in-law, Judah.

Whatever our circumstance, marital status or age, I have come to believe that God loves and cares for us as single mothers and for others like us.

Single Divorced Christian Mother, I am talking to you, in particular. Take encouragement and strength from 1 Peter 5:17, which reads: 'Casting all your anxieties on Him, because He cares for you.' Nothing, *absolutely nothing*, can separate you from the love of God. Nothing from then until now and forever has separated me from Him, and this is your birthright, too. Jesus paid it all: my sins, my mistakes, your sins, your mistakes… all nailed to the cross. Paid in full.

Learning Points

I have talked about my experiences and observations as an MRM (Married, Re-singled and Mature) woman of God. One day I hope to add a second 'R', to cover a section on Remarriage, so it will become MRMR. I am looking forward to that with healthy expectation, but for now, let me share with you seven of my key learning points from my MRM journey that I believe you will also find valuable in your own:

1. **Uncover areas where there may be idolatry**
   Idolatry simply put is anything that takes priority over God Himself. Your idol may not be your marriage; it could be anything. The learning point is to reflect, review, recognise where (if at all) something you have may be lingering as an idol and deal with it. Ask the Holy Spirit to reveal to you if there is anything in your life that has taken your time and attention away from worshipping God.

Matthew 6:33 NLT
"Seek the Kingdom of God above all else, and live righteously, and He will give you everything you need."

2. **Mask**
   Ditch the mask and the need to keep up appearances, and therefore not showing up as your authentic self. The One, whose opinion matters, knows exactly what you are going through. Be vulnerable and transparent with our God; it is *His* opinion of you that counts. Stop and imagine, just for a moment, where your life looks good to all on the outside, *but stinks to God*. He is waiting to help. Cry out to Him and He will come running.

3. **Take time to rediscover who you are in Christ**
   Search the Scriptures. There are many providing confirmation of who you are. Here are two to start you off:

   Ephesians 2:10 NLT
   'For we are God's masterpiece. He has created us anew in Christ Jesus, so we can do the good things He planned for us long ago.'

   2 Corinthians 5:17
   'Therefore, if anyone is in Christ, he is a new creation; old things have passed away; behold, all things have become new.'

4. **Forgiveness**
   This is crucial if you want to move forward after the trauma of grief and loss. Forgive your ex-spouse, partner, fiancé(e) or even deceased spouse. Forgive God and, in all this, make sure you also forgive yourself.

   Colossians 3:12-13 NIV
   'Therefore, as God's chosen people, holy and dearly loved, clothe yourselves with compassion, kindness, humility, gentleness and patience. Bear with each other and

forgive one another if any of you has a grievance against someone. Forgive as the Lord forgave you.'

5. **Raise your expectations**
   Your past is over — whether it was good or not so good — so expect better for your future. Be intentional about the steps you need to take to move forward into your 'better'. Know that God has amazing plans for you, so you have a future and need to have a hope for that future.

   Jeremiah 29:11 AMP
   '"For I know the plans and thoughts that I have for you," says the Lord, "plans for peace and well-being and not for disaster, to give you a future and a hope."'

6. **Take responsibility**
   Getting rid of the blame game; own up to your errors; learn the lessons; get the healing and cleansing available from God, then prepare to move on.

   1 John 1:9
   'If we confess our sins, He is faithful and just to forgive us our sins and to cleanse us from all unrighteousness.'

7. **Dealing with ungodly spirits**
   When we are dealing with ungodly spirits that come out of grief and loss, it is important to call upon the Holy Spirit, the Spirit of all truth, to help you renounce and cancel all relationship with:

   a. **The spirit of heaviness (Isaiah 61:3)** covering a broken heart, defeat, rejection, despair, hopelessness, mourning, loss, self-pity, regret, guilt, shame, depression, suicidal thoughts, depression, low self-esteem and discouragement, unforgiveness.

b. The spirit of fear (2 Timothy 1:7) — Fearfulness manifests itself in various ways. This is fear of the unknown, the future, rejection, abandonment, inadequacy, failure, death, comparisons, loneliness and shame. Breaking your relationships with fear will empower you — like it did me — with the ability to walk in the love, peace and joy God has made readily available when you ask. No matter what you have gone through or are going through, I urge you to ask God for your unique and divine revelation of His perfect love for you. Remember, perfect love has the ability to cast out fear (1 John 4:18).

c. The spirit of infirmity (Luke 13:11-13) — Never underestimate the kind of infirmities unresolved grief and loss can cause in your life, such as unexplained illnesses and pains, weaknesses, lack of finances, no peace of mind, sleeplessness, sluggishness, clumsiness, tension headaches, nightmares, persecution, etc. If you identify any of these, ask God for the gift of healing and that He grants you wholeness. Also, replace your fears with wonderful thoughts in accordance with Philippians 4:8 NLT: 'And now, dear brothers and sisters, one final thing. Fix your thoughts on what is true, and honourable, and right, and pure, and lovely, and admirable. Think about things that are excellent and worthy of praise.'

The Finishing Line — No Excuses

Whatever category of 'single' we have found ourselves in, there's no excuse not to be and do what God has called us to. Our mission and mandate from God are not dependant upon our marital status, or on whether we have children or not. God expects us to invest in the gifts He has bestowed upon us, and to represent Him well in the spheres of influence He has placed us into.

Looking back, I am wondering why I was so anxious and afraid about my future with my daughters in the first place. They were seven and four at the time; they are now 24 and 21. Has it been easy? No, but as CeCe Winans says: "It was worth it." God has proven Himself over the years that there has been a purpose for everything, even the things in my life that broke my heart and looked like they would sift the very breath out of me.

In 2012, I set up my first ministry – Believe and Live Again — a Restorative Coaching and Reinvention Mentoring Service, helping women of faith and female professionals to move 'from we to me'; heal from the pain, and reinvent themselves during and after divorce.

In 2017, I published my first best-selling book, *'Reinvent You! How to Move from We to Me After Divorce'*. In 2018, I set up the Reinvent You Experience Coaching Service to help women stuck after the trauma of a life transition to become unstuck and create profitable legacies and, in December 2018, I set up a charity, the Reinvent YOU After Abuse Foundation, to bring healing, recovery and financial independence to victims and survivors of domestic violence and abuse, especially economic abuse.

I used to feel bashful about all these accomplishments, but today I boast in the Lord, because out of the lemons of my divorce and single motherhood, He guided and taught me how to make lemonade. Since 2012 I have worked with and impacted thousands of women around the world, and in the process, some have come to faith and many others have renewed their faith.

You may be reading this and perhaps cannot even begin to understand or make sense of your own life's experiences, but take God at His Word and choose to believe that even the bad things in your life that may have been meant for evil, God in His mercy, love and compassion means it for good, and in the fullness of His time, He fulfils His promise uncovering that good, that lemonade.

My sisters and brothers, have faith in Him, seek Him out in your darkest moments, and receive the blessed assurance and comfort that good will come.

Much love, hope and God's blessings
Dr Zina Arinze

INFORMATION ABOUT THE WRITER

Zina Arinze is a woman who wears many hats, including lawyer, author, radio broadcaster and talk show host, international transformational speaker, coach, multi-award-winning community leader, successful serial entrepreneur and the founder of Believe and Live Again, the Post-Divorce Lifestyle Coaching, Abuse Recovery and Reinvention Mentoring service for female professionals, women of faith, businesswomen and female entrepreneurs from around the globe.

You can connect with Zina at www.facebook.com/zinaarinze

Email: zinaarinze@believeandliveagain.com

FAMOUS LAST WORDS

by Roney Henderson

Introduction

It was 2020, the year a crisis became a pandemic. It wasn't expected; there was no sign that everyone could see and take note that the world was about to change. It was a 'suddenly' situation. Suddenly we had to work from home; suddenly we had to wear masks in public; suddenly all public places were closed; suddenly we couldn't visit friends or relatives… But this is not my first experience of a pandemic.

I am no longer 30. Not even 40. Not even 45 and I am single — a state in which I have spent my entire life. Is it by choice? Was it my decision? If not, then at whose feet can I lay the blame? I am an involuntarily single, and COVID-19 for me was the second pandemic in my life. The first is being part of the Black Caribbean Church here in Britain, where the ratio of single Black men to Black women can be as high as 7 to 1 in some congregations.

I know many single Black women, with pent-up anger and frustration, which are covered up with their fake Pan Am smiles and their professions, which afford them a mortgage, car, holidays and restaurants. Like me, many of them have never given birth, are infertile or just childless.

Sometimes my mind runs riot. Why didn't I do this, why didn't I do that? How did I let this happen? Why was I a good girl who followed the rules? Why didn't I leave the church for a while, have a baby and come back? Why did I believe what I was told? Why did I allow myself to be lied to for so many years? (And yes, the lies are many.) Why didn't I see my life of singleness coming? What was I so occupied with that I was blindsided?

Every now and then I'm angry — not at the world, not at men and not at God. I am angry at the Black Church. How can a movement, started by twelve men and aimed at the world, now be dominated by women? I find it exceedingly difficult to understand how any male church leader is happy to lead a congregation that, at times, is more than 90% female. A male friend once told me that the roles of men in the Muslim faith is very clear, but he hasn't experienced that same type of clarity as a man in the Black Church, because the messages are directed towards women.

There are many phrases, some are even Scriptures, that I now think of as 'Famous Last Words'. They are continuously said to single women who attend Black churches, either at a singles' event or during a conversation about marriage with singles as the topic.

These Famous Last Words, including the scriptural ones, are being used as a form of subliminal messaging and mind-conditioning tool. Like a slow, dripping tap, these words slowly erode a woman's confidence and free thinking, and she is unaware of what is happening to her mentally until it's too late. This inevitably changes her mindset, positioning her for involuntary singlehood,[1] and involuntary celibacy (being single and unable to find a marriage partner for sexual relations).

1. **NOT READY FOR MARRIAGE**

   "Are you ready for marriage? Are you *sure*? Because many people think they're ready but are not. Marriage isn't easy and it's not for everybody." I have heard these famous words at every singles' conference event I have attended — and I have been to many and even spoken at a few. After more than 10 years of boycotting singles' conferences, in 2021 I attended a Zoom event. These famous words were once again uttered by a married panelist. There was a time I believed these words. I took them home. I memorised them. I prayed against those words, for them to be out of my life. I was in my 30s and unmarried, which in my mind meant I needed fixing. I believed I wasn't ready and was far from a woman prepared for marriage. I had to change. The problem was I couldn't determine what needed changing; what was

1 Donnelly and Burgess, The decision to remain in an involuntarily celibate relationship, https://link.springer.com/article/10.1007/s12144-016-9478-3 (2008)

wrong with me, and how I was going to get it 'fixed', so that God in His infinite wisdom would consider me suitable for marriage and reveal who my husband is in a dream.

OK. Time to fast and pray. That's the answer. I cannot see the problem I have, so I am going to go down the spiritual route to fix me for marriage. Fasting and prayer will send me a man — and one who speaks in tongues, because that is proof of a godly man. The archetype of a good 'church guy', i.e., Christian man, is one who prays with his wife and loves her as Christ does the Church. I fasted and prayed many times over the years. Still single. No proposal. Not even a serious relationship gone wrong. Just nothing. So *that* didn't work.

2. GOD IS YOUR HUSBAND

Oh, this apparently is what the single life is about. "God is your Husband." I don't fully understand why I, and probably millions of other women, have been taught about marriage in a negative way and have been left to think of God as our Husband. It is baffling to say the least. Why in the Black Church is God the single women's Husband? Who is the single man's wife? I have never heard a minister or anyone say: "God is your wife." No, no, that isn't said to the men.

We the women are the target. Everything is aimed at the women in church, including messages to keep them from leaving and actively pursuing marriage elsewhere. I believe saying this presents a form of hopelessness to an already desperate group of women who are looking in the Church for their ideal partner. God is not my Husband, and I will never regard Him as such. I see Him as my heavenly Father.

3. BE NOT UNEQUALLY YOKED

You cannot marry an unbeliever. Who says so? Well, the Bible says 'be not unequally yoked.... What fellowship has light with darkness?'[2]. This is the most celebrated, and incorrectly overused, quoted text to women in Black churches. In fact,

2 KJV Bible, 2 Corinthians 6:14

I have never heard this quote used for anything else other than to make sure we know not to marry someone who is not considered a believer — a non-Christian. According to the NIV Bible, the text refers to 'Christian believers cooperating with false teachers who are, in reality, servants of Satan'[3]. This Scripture is regularly thrown in the face of the women who are 'desperately seeking Mike' within the four walls of their church or online. What hope can they feel when everything spoken about marriage always has an element of fear attached?

4. **HE THAT FINDETH A WIFE**

"Ladies, you do not look for a man. The Bible is clear: 'He, who finds a wife, finds a good thing'[4]. God will send the man to you. You do not need to do the looking. Just pray and seek the Lord, he (the man) will come." This Scripture is about a man finding a suitable wife and the blessing she brings to his life. Looking back, it seems ridiculous that we swallowed and fell for this — hook, line and sinker. We never really questioned our leaders; we just believed what they said and, for the most part, just followed their instructions. Well, not *every*one followed, because there is always the exception to the rule, and there have and always will be women in church getting pregnant outside of marriage.

Imagine a church community of 5000, of which 4000 are singles (aged 16 and over), typically made up of 1200 men and 2800 women. There are 1600 women who will have to expect a husband from elsewhere, because the numbers reveal there is no man available to find them in this particular church.

5. **WAIT ON THE LORD**

If ever a saying has been used without proper explanation and context to single women in the Black Church, then this

[3] NIV Study Bible (1985) Notes, p 1736

[4] NKJV Proverbs 18:22

is it: 'Wait on the Lord'[5]. This is what the average unmarried, female churchgoer above the age of 40 will have heard countless times — probably because she may have been passively waiting for her husband to manifest.

I'm going to take a wild guess here and say that the manifestation of the man is the actual event and, because that has not happened, many women have taken no action to secure a husband. They're still waiting, standing in the 'still' position, looking who's coming through the church doors or at the next big worship conference, and ignoring the man on the bus or in the Post Office queue. A friend of mine met her husband whilst in a car at the traffic lights. He was in a car in the next lane. They exchanged numbers. Another friend met her husband in a supermarket aisle.

We believed in the waiting because we know God answers prayers. After we've waited for an answer, we were told to keep waiting, because bad things happen to those who don't. Well, we waited, and nothing good has come of it for many of us because we are still single. The house, the car, money in the bank, great girlfriends, lovely wardrobe, terrific holidays… But still single.

Waiting is an action word. You wait with expectation; waiting is an action which you have carried out and so expect a result. It really is a sad indictment that many women continue to wait passively, and become bitter, frustrated and angry in the waiting, and then realise it's too late to have children. There are fewer men who are waiting for the older woman, especially when younger women are readily available to them.

6. NOT EVERYONE IS GOING TO GET MARRIED

Another phrase I'm exhausted to hear was said at the opening of a large Singles' Valentine's Day women's church event. "Not all of you are going to get married." Who was she speaking to? Who are these women who are not going

5 KJV Psalm 27:14

to get married? Can someone please point them out to me, because I have yet to meet a single person who believes or knows they are not getting married. I'm not thinking about the divorcees who dare not darken the marriage path again, or those who have bitter experiences in relationships and have made up their minds. I want to know which single woman, who wants to get married, believes she will not be getting married. I want to meet someone in their 30s and 40s who knows this for certain. Some women in their 50s and 60s may not know, and furthermore may now decide not to be so bothered about marriage anymore, but who knows what can happen? So, if there was ever a cop-out statement, then this is it.

The reason why most women attending a Black church won't have the opportunity for marriage is because they are looking in an environment where single men are few. The Black Church does not focus on men (even though society would be better off if it did). Its focus is on women, which means men have very little interest in attending church and so, for those women who can only see themselves marrying a Christian, many of them will become the saying, 'Not everyone is going to get married', and realise too late that they missed out on other opportunities outside of the four walls of their church.

7. SINGLENESS IS A GIFT

The apostle Paul laid down the foundation for the Christian Church. It appears that Paul was single and very happy being so, to the point where he says he wished we 'all were like him' [6]. I came across an online article, '5 Gifts of Being Single', one of which included not being in a terrible marriage[7]. The same author also wrote another article on

6 KJV Bible, 1 Corinthians 6:7

7 Mark Ballenger, Biblical Singleness: 5 Gifts of Being Single According to the Bible, https://applygodsword.com/biblical-singleness-5-gifts-of-being-single-according-to-the-bible/ (2008)

the three ways God was leading him and his now wife to be married[8].

This is another of those sayings that is told to singles, by people who are married. I mean, if you haven't espoused the single life, why are you promoting that life to single women? This is never said to men. What is the 'gift of singleness', when you want to be someone's wife and have children? Doesn't the Scripture also say that the older women are to teach the younger woman how to be good wives to their husbands, to be busy at home, kind, subject to their husbands, self-controlled and pure?[9]

There is a time for singleness and a time to be married. It can be very painful to be in an environment where singleness is constantly promoted, and what you really want is intimacy with a man. What you really want is to give birth to another life. What you really want is to be held by someone of the opposite sex. What you really want is to be taken out to dinner by a man and know that it doesn't end there. But no, in the Black Church singleness is a gift that just keeps on giving.

8. THE MOST YOU DO FOR JESUS IN CHURCH

In most Black churches, women comprise the majority of the congregation. This means women keep the church going financially, spiritually, relationally and physically. Most churches have one or two services on a Sunday, a midweek Bible class and a prayer evening. Many women will attend all of them, plus run or assist in other departments, such as administration, women's department, cleaning, catering, hospitality, etc. Some women end up having no social life because they're all about church and, unfortunately, it can be difficult for them to break the habit.

8 Mark Ballenger, How God Told Us to Get Married, https://applygodsword.com/how-god-told-us-to-get-married-mark-and-bethany-ballenger/ (2008)

9 KJV Bible, Titus 2:3-5

In some churches, women feel pressed upon to be at all events, because otherwise they are questioned by leaders or assistants — or even other members — as to why they were not at a particular event, even though they hold no office in the church. There can be times when a woman just wants to breathe but is made to feel guilty breathing.

The vision indeed has been given to the pastor of how the church should be. The members support that vision — sometimes at the cost of their personal life and dreams (given to them by the Most High). Some leaders only really care about their own vision, and although they will encourage members to have one for themselves, do most of these members actually find the time to implement their vision? No. Because they are either *in* church or on their way *to* church or doing something *for* the church. This has caused some marriages to fail, because some wives place the needs of the pastor and the church above their husbands and family. Scripture talks of when helping the least of your fellow man, it's as if you did it for Him[10], but many have got this twisted and are sacrificing their husbands, family and homes and treating *them* as 'the least' and instead are treating their church and pastors as 'the most'.

9. THE ACTIONS OF RUTH – THEY LEAVE

I once had a discussion with a minister. I can still remember the venue, the surroundings and when it took place — the reason being that in the conversation this pastor unknowingly revealed to me how some ministers think. Whilst our discussion was in a crowded restaurant with music playing in the background, we were able to hear each other clearly. I spoke to him about my frustration with the Church's attitude towards the women's singleness issue. He listened intently and then said the five words that summed up the bigger part of the matter, of which many women

10 KJV Bible Matthew 25:40

are not aware. He said: "The problem is they leave." I was confused; I had no idea what he was talking about or what he meant by that statement. Those were the last words he said to me before moving on to speak to someone else. I sat down and pondered for a while on what he meant. Eventually, it hit me like a ton of bricks as I sat in the chair, shocked and amazed at what I had just been told.

Most women, when they marry a man from another church, become a member of their husband's congregation. A few weeks later I mentioned the conversation I'd had with the pastor to another male minister. He agreed that leaders don't want certain members to leave their church, as it is hard to replace a good worker.

I was shocked on both counts. The question must be asked: Are leaders *intentionally* being negative about marriage to their members, who are predominantly women, because they don't want them to leave? Am I in an environment where the subtleties of mind control, similar to subliminal advertising, have been used to keep the majority of church women where they are and in a state of singleness? Does a local pastor really want to have a ministry, where women are getting married and no longer have church activities as their number one priority, but their first commitment is to their husbands, homes and families?

Many of these women were brought up in church, at a time when you were considered holy not only by your faith but also by your appearance and behaviour. There was extraordinarily little room to manoeuvre or to just be your own plain self.

In terms of expressing an interest in the opposite sex, there were no gentle flirtations allowed, no dropping of the handkerchief, no brushing against another person to get their attention, or slipping the phone number into a hand when walking down the aisle to give an offering… So many women were fairly rigid in their approach to a relationship with the opposite sex. Professor Menelaos Apostolou, in his study[11] of 1228 men and women, found that participants who scored low in flirting capacity, i.e. capacity to perceive signals of interest and mating effort, were more likely to be involuntarily single than in an intimate relationship, and experienced longer spells of singlehood.

I once met a woman who had taken on board everything her church had told her about personal relationships, to the point that she refused to smile at men in case they thought she was interested in them. She didn't want to give the wrong impression but, at the same time, she was looking for a husband.

In conclusion, there is a saying that time is a teacher, and what the over-40 women in Black churches *now* know is that your future partner is someone you have to actively pursue — just like a career or anything else you want in life.

I have called this essay Famous Last Words because over the years these were some of the words I'd taken away from the singles' events I attended. They say hindsight is always twenty-twenty, meaning that it's only when you look back at an event you get the complete understanding about what happened.

Looking back, I see that the Black Church I attended had a lot less freedom than it has today. Like thousands of others, the choices I made seemed right at the time, however, I didn't stop long enough to make the steps for the life I wanted but continued along the same path. So where does the blame truly lie for me and thousands of other women? Initially it lies with the Black Church, however, at some point we are all required to drop our fears, take the necessary, bold steps and reach out for the greatest gift: Love.

11 Menelaos Apostolou, Involuntary singlehood and its causes: The effects of flirting capacity, mating effort, choosiness and capacity to perceive signals of interest, https://www.sciencedirect.com/science/article/abs/pii/S0191886921001574, (2021)

INFORMATION ABOUT THE WRITER

Roney Henderson has been a member of a Black church all her life. A project manager and former gospel events and music promoter, she loves film and was the Chair of the South Norwood and Thornton Heath free film festival from 2014 to 2016. On weekends, she is a script supervisor on short films and will be launching the FAB film festival in 2022 for lovers of Inspirational and Spiritual films. In 2021 she was part of the production team for the *People Get Ready* vodcast about the legendary gospel music series that was aired on ITV and Channel 4.

Connect with Roney at www.facebook.com/roney.henderson

Email: roneyhenderson@aol.com

MAKING THE MOST OF THE SINGLE LIFE

by Shenelle Markland

"You love God, you're faithful and you're beautiful. I don't get it. Why are you still single?"

"You're 30 now, you need to hurry up and get married if you want children! Are you speaking to anyone?"

"How comes you're not married?"

"You keep attending weddings, when is *yours*?"

Heard any of these comments before?

I surely have! These are just a few of the questions I've been asked over the last few years by Christians who have good intentions, and who genuinely desire to see me get married and start my very own family.

Whilst I appreciate the many good intentions and desires people have for me, we sometimes fail to realise that these very same questions can pressurise single Christian women into thinking that being a single Christian woman is inadequate. These same questions can unconsciously create the misconception that one isn't complete or whole until they are married. These same questions can be a factor that lead individuals to settle and get into relationships they should never have entered into, simply due to feeling pressured.

Sometimes it's so easy to place emphasis on what we don't have, and overlook the blessings we have already. Whilst I desire to do life with a significant other and start my own family, **I am content during this season of singleness, and see this season of my life as an opportunity to focus on prioritising my relationship with God and working on developing myself (with God's help) to be the best version of me.**

It's easy to compare myself to others, and seeing the beautiful wedding proposals and those picture-perfect families on Instagram can leave me wondering "When will it be *my* turn?" I remind myself there is a season for everything, and during this season I'm in, it's vital I focus on what I already have and use this time to develop, appreciate, grow and enjoy life.

So how do I enjoy and use the time of this crucial season of my life wisely?

1. **Strive to put God first and realise that true completion comes from God**
   "But seek ye first the Kingdom of God, and His righteousness; and all these things shall be added unto you" (Matthew 6:33).

   It is my ultimate priority to seek God, and to continually develop a deeper relationship with Him through prayer, reading His Word and being a true follower of Christ. This surpasses all other desires and, whilst at times I struggle to put God first, I am reassured that God will bless me for prioritising Him and His Kingdom.

   It's also very important to realise that only God can truly complete us and fill any void in our lives. Whilst it is absolutely fine to desire a significant other, a family, a successful career, financial security, etc, none of these things can really make us feel whole. We can have all our desires and still feel a lack, dissatisfaction and a thirst for more! Only Christ can satisfy us; Jesus Christ provides for our needs, fulfils our desires, and provides the joy and satisfaction we truly seek.

   'Jesus said to them: "I am the Bread of life; whoever comes to Me shall not hunger, and whoever believes in Me shall never thirst"' (John 6:35). So thinking that a spouse will satisfy the void in your life will leave you disappointed.

2. **Work on being the best version of me**
   When you're single, it is the perfect opportunity to work on being the best version of yourself. Of course, self-

development should be ongoing but during this season you have more time to do so.

Self-development and character pruning! Why wait until you meet your spouse to start working on yourself? The time is now! Every day is an opportunity to try to be more like Jesus Christ.

As we go through the process of sanctification on a daily basis, I try my best to ask the Holy Spirit to help me be more like Christ and prune away all the unhealthy/ungodly characteristics that reside within me. It's important we use this time to invest in ourselves!

Use this time to develop good healthy habits, undertake courses, or develop skills that can support our career progression; go to those conferences/talks that will develop you spiritually, emotionally, personally, socially and financially. Learn that skill!

I have a pretty busy life, but I value the importance of self-growth and working on being the person God has called me to be. It's my desire that when God places my future spouse into my life, I will be as whole as possible (of course, there is always room for self-development), and add value to my spouse's life.

3. **Spend time with family and friends**

I thoroughly enjoy spending precious time with the loved ones I already have. Spending time with my family and friends and creating priceless memories truly bring joy to my heart.

I personally believe that your family is your first ministry, and we ought to prioritise our families above serving in a ministry at church or in the community. Sometimes I find it hard to balance the day-to-day busyness of life, but nothing beats those spontaneous gatherings with family members, where you eat, laugh and have a great time.

If we don't make time to appreciate and spend quality time with the family we already have, will we know how to when we start our own family? And, let's face it, when you're in a relationship you might not have as much time to spend with your friends as you did when you were single, so make sure you maximise this time! I'm a real foodie, so I love dressing up with my friends and going to an aesthetically pleasing restaurant, experiencing new activities and, of course, going on those girly holidays!

4. **Serve in church**

Serve! Serve! Serve! Anyone who knows me, knows I'm an advocate for serving in church. Jesus exemplified servanthood, so we should too! We are called to serve, and there are so many benefits to serving.

It has helped me to develop my relationship with Christ, as I'm surrounded by other believers who encourage, pray, correct and do life with me, as we serve together in ministry.

Serving in church helped me to find my calling. I volunteered to serve within the Children's ministry and, through serving the children, I realised God had called me to teach. Having the opportunity to impart God's love, truth and Word into the children and seeing their spiritual and personal growth is such a blessing and honour to witness.

Through serving the children, I have learnt and been taught so much. Serving helps to support your church's vision and mission, and it's such a beautiful thing to witness your church growing and fulfilling God's plans. Serving in ministry can also help to ignite and highlight gifts and callings.

5. **Enjoy yourself!**

Enjoy your life! Do the exciting things you want to do (as long as it's pleasing to God!). Travel, explore and simply have fun! You will never have this time again!

But let's be real. Being single isn't always easy, and sometimes you question whether your time will ever

come. What do you do if you find yourself struggling with being single?

a. **Tell God**
It's important that we are open with God about our feelings towards being single. Pour your heart out to God and take it to Him in prayer. God cares about our innermost thoughts and feelings, and will comfort us when we are feeling low.

b. **Speak to a trusted friend who is also single**
Don't struggle alone! If you're feeling lonely or are finding it difficult during this season of singleness, connect with other single people as a source of encouragement. Share experiences, struggles and advice on how to navigate through this season.

c. **Be proactive**
If you really want to meet someone, what practical steps are you taking to meet new people? Are you engaging in opportunities to meet, speak or connect with new people? Are you working through any issues/experiences or traumas that could hinder you from being available to enter into a relationship? Ask yourself, are you being proactive? If you really want to meet someone, is there anything that you can do to help the process?

Whilst there will be times when being single isn't easy, I truly believe that if you use this season to spend time with God; work on your personal growth and development; appreciate and spend time with your family and loved ones, as well as serve, you will be able to embrace and maximise this current season of singleness.

INFORMATION ABOUT THE WRITER

Shenelle Markland is a primary school teacher, Sunday school leader and school governor. She has a passion for children/young people and strives to support children/young people in flourishing to become the best versions of themselves and, most importantly, who God has called them to be. Shenelle loves God, people, food, and fashion and in her spare time enjoys walking and trying out new activities and experiences.

You can connect with Shenelle at www.instagram.com/sjmm08/

Email: shenellemarkland@gmail.com

SINGLE, HORNY AND SANCTIFIED

by Cherlene Wilson

I know that title caught your attention! The boldness, the audacity, and the seeming paradox. I have often wondered why we in Christendom can get so offended or feel awkward by what is true for many of us in our singleness.

When looking deeper into this topic, into my own inner work, and coaching countless people about managing their purity, I have discovered there is freedom that comes when we accept and embrace this truth, rather than denying it. The opposite is also true. When we choose to suppress the reality of our sex drives and the biological expressions our bodies present — all whilst we are passionately loving Jesus — we keep ourselves in bondage and in a place where the fruit of grace (supernatural empowerment) may encounter resistance to abound.

I would like to take you on a journey: sharing my reflections, the results of emotional violations, the victories, and what I have been doing to maintain over 14 years of abstinence. Yes, you read right. From years of observation and decades of personal experience, I feel the Church on a whole has done a great injustice by telling us what not to do, while failing to teach us the practicals of how not to do it. Many methods of encouraging sexual purity have been laced with fear, judgement and condemnation to steer us in the 'right direction'.

In many cases, people have ended up asking God to take away their libido, believing that sexual desire is innately bad. Poor messaging has often resulted in people living sexually frustrated in isolation with porn, masturbation and sex. What I have come to learn is that this leaves many of us wading through guilt and shame, living double lives, and falling short of making great choices.

I believe all these states are completely unnecessary if we learn how to live emotionally honest lives, implement *effective* tools, and live authentically in our God-given identities. We must come to an understanding that the villain isn't our sex drive or sexual appetite; it is the inability to *manage* the desires *effectively*. With that in mind, it is my aim for you to walk away from this chapter feeling freer, seen, and empowered at whatever stage of life you are in.

When you think of purity, what comes to mind? No sex before marriage? That it's an unobtainable feat? Inner conflict, hard to connect to, or even an internal eye roll? I can understand that. 'Purity' can come across elusively cloaked in 'isms' from the pulpit, with action Scriptures, like 'Resist the devil and he will flee from you' (James 4:7-9 NKJV), and 'For it is better to marry than to burn with passion' (1 Corinthians 7:9 NKJV). Here is what I have come to tell you today: purity is *not* just a state of being, it is also a state of *heart*.

We can scream abstinence all we like but be perverted in our minds and in our intentions. We can be abstinent (meaning no penetration), but what is *actually* happening is 'slipping and sliding' with tongues, hands and toys. We can be lust-filled or engaged in seducing the opposite sex with our words and our actions, while our hearts are secretly postured to objectify and sexualise our brothers and sisters. We burn brain calories entertaining vain imaginations, when we know they ought to be cast down under the authority of God. Hear me well, there is no shade or judgement if you are in any of those areas in your life right now. I have lived there in my past, so I feel you. If you are camping in this place however, I would like to hand you a skeleton key to set you free from the prison you may have put yourself into. The key is to 'call a spade a spade' and see it for what it is, so that grace can be imparted in you, and the spirit of liberty released into your situation.

As a 40-something single lady, I am in the age bracket where a woman's sex drive is at its peak! Listen, God Himself has had to 'be a fence' *and* take the wheel, believe me!

Navigating the journey from the battlefield to the marriage bed has been tear-filled and frustrating at times, but still, at the core of it, conviction functions as an anchor. A life of abstinence is not just because of what God has asked of me, but it's also because I genuinely want it for myself and to give the fruit of it to my family.

As much as I may have desired sexual intimacy and to fully act on it in my singlehood, it is too costly, and here is why. Have you ever thought about how much we hear the message on breaking generational curses? And how rarely, if ever, do we hear sermons asking us whether it is possible that our current heart posture, mindset and/or behaviour are actively creating the curses that will need to be broken by the generations that come after us? *#selah.* I want to ensure that I take time now to do the work: 1. to be an asset to my future husband, and 2. to ensure transgenerational trauma isn't gifted to my children in the womb.

Living in the tension between values and human desire for intimacy and connection can be one of the greatest conflicts of our souls. I'll be honest and admit that over the years I have tried to negotiate with God and even wondered if, just for a moment, He would engage in amnesia while I compromise my values and fulfil my desires!

It has been difficult keeping hope alive, when there is a deep desire for affection — especially while witnessing what feels like a dearth of Christian men who do not share the same convictions; who are nursing post-divorce trauma; who want to 'try-before-they-buy', or who are generally unhappy in life. Witnessing failed marriages and multiple stories of infidelities, you can understand why. As a result, compromising and lowering my standards was a jungle I considered trekking through.

My heart began to grow sick in the waiting and I was becoming lax in guarding my heart. I have found, on rare occasions, that my speech would betray me. My appetite was changing and expanding to welcome conversations I wouldn't typically have — the kind of conversations that start to sow seeds... You know the ones: the ones you use 'accidentally on purpose' to get your emotional needs met. We *can* go ahead and sow those seeds, but we must remember we are never in control of the harvest they will produce.

I could sense myself sliding along a path that could have concluded with me telling you I had given away 14 years of abstinence. Things got to a point where I had to be honest with myself. Was I going to continue to violate my conscience; allow my integrity to slowly erode; compromise my purpose and delay my destiny? Or was I going to put on my 'big girl' pants, do what I knew was right and cut it off at the root? We all get to a point in our situations where we are faced with making the decision. I can tell you this, making what seems to be a sacrifice is going to pay you dividends in your future. It may not seem like it now, but believe me, if there is one thing I have learnt, God will give us grace. Ask Holy Spirit to help you — even if your voice shakes, knees get wobbly and heart races — to have that conversation; you will be fine in the end.

There were several steps that have graced me to arrive at this place, but first I would like to share a little of my history with you.

Exposure to sexuality happened at the age of nine, when a family member attempted to have sex with me as a part of his initiation into a school gang. Aged 14, I was groomed and subsequently raped by a youth evangelist in the church I attended. Upon trying to share what had happened to me, I was labelled a Jezebel and made to feel like I was in the wrong, even though the man was the adult. That led me to leaving the church and finding solace in gang life and gang culture. The trauma of what happened locked my emotions and behaviour into self-destructive patterns, mindsets, cycles and an appetite for sex.

Imagine that being the relational starting point of an early teen, at the same time as loving and desiring God. Add membership to a Pentecostal denomination to the mix, peppered with judgement, and condemnation maintained by stigma and fear, there were *very* few people I could share this juxtaposition with.

As a Christian woman, holding two truths — that I love sex and love God — was a very scary tightrope to walk across, and most certainly one I measured before sharing publicly. But it is the truth. Owning this fact was one of the most freeing things I have ever done in this context. It was this admittance that birthed the freedom to regard this area of my life with grace, self-compassion and understanding. I had given myself the freedom I needed to be honest and not expect the worst from myself and God. It was a process, though — one that I would like to start you on if you are in the place of needing to.

In 2007 I came to the realisation that I am not a sinner saved by grace, but rather a sinner saved by grace to *become* a saint. My identity was not the 'old man' — because 'he' died in accordance with Romans 6 — but rather, it was this fundamental belief that says when I gave my life to Christ, *I* died, was buried and was resurrected in Him. That same power that raised Jesus from the dead resides in you and I. When we realise this, sin doesn't get to dictate to us; on the contrary, we get to dictate to it.

So what happened in me? An identity shift, a heart shift and the renewing of my mind began. I realised I was fighting from a place of victory, not trying to obtain victory. I began to understand that focusing on the pursuit of being righteous, nurturing a righteous heart posture and righteous thinking was the thing to do. That gave me the conviction to look at men as God's sons, as kings and as someone's husband. This applied revelation was a gamechanger for me — and could be for you too.

What if you believed you were the righteousness of God and that your heart was innately postured towards goodness? How would that change this area of your life?

With a background in psychology and criminology, for many years I have been fascinated by the heart and human behaviour. We often believe our behaviour is influenced by our minds. That is partly true, however there is scientific research and evidence that conclude that each one of us has a 'heart-brain', otherwise known as a 'little brain'. It has approximately 40,000 sensory neurons[12] sending information to the brain, and is 5,000 times more powerful than the cranial brain[13]. The 'little brain' can make an independent decision, *bypassing* the cerebral cortex which is associated with

12 https://pubmed.ncbi.nlm.nih.gov/31728781/

13 https://www.psychologytoday.com/intl/blog/building-the-habit-hero/202011/the-hearts-electromagnetic-field-is-your-superpower

higher level processes such as consciousness, thought, emotion, reasoning, language and memory[14].

When we were being developed in our mother's womb, our hearts were formed before our brains. The heart is literally the starting point of everything we do. It sends more information to the brain than the brain ever does to the heart and can affect your emotional experiences. That being the case, it would be fair to say that both physically and metaphorically, taking care of the heart is paramount if we are going to live fruitful, healthy and emotionally successful lives. These findings further confirm the importance of 'Above all else, guard your heart, for everything you do flows from it' (Proverbs 4:23 NIV).

Our first and most important relationship after God is the one we have with ourselves. So how do we guard our heart? By nurturing it. You may be wondering, 'How do I start working on my relationship with my heart?' This is what has helped me.

Reverse-engineer your behaviour. Take a step backwards from your behaviour and observe it objectively. Next, pinpoint what you are thinking or believing. Ask yourself, 'What narrative am I believing about (fill the gap)?', eg. about a relationship or about yourself. Note that down. Then ask, 'What lies am I believing about (fill the gap)?' Then ask, 'What is the truth?' After that, we will have a clearer view of our heart.

Earlier I mentioned that my heart grew sick, as I started to lose hope in relationships and the possibility of marriage. The narrative I began to believe about myself was "There must be something wrong with me that I cannot see, and that's the reason I am yet to be married.' The lies led to further lies: 'I need to lower my standards to be found' and 'I will never be found by a man who shares my values and who fully accepts all of who I am.' My heart's condition was one of hopelessness. I was believing the narrative and lies so much, I couldn't find hope. The truth is, my king *is* out there, looking for me as much as I am looking out for him.

14 https://courses.lumenlearning.com/wmopen-psychology/chapter/outcome-parts-of-the-brain/

Over time, as we grow in our relationship with our heart, we will know what our heart's condition is and give it what it needs. It will take practice, self-awareness and time, so please give yourself grace. If you are feeling condemnation, eg. wanting to hide from God, consistently beating yourself up and feeling shame for your choices, it is the enemy speaking to you and trying to keep you far from God.

God is a loving Father and the One who outrageously loves you. If you are feeling conviction, eg. remorse (a deep regret of actions taken against your spiritual values), please know this is Holy Spirit attempting to draw you closer to Him. He convicts us of righteousness and reminds us who we are and the right thing to do. So, what do we need to do? We need to take responsibility for our heart health, and I would encourage you to seek help with a sex addiction therapist, get purity coaching or emotional healing.

Getting ferociously practical will be essential. Creating a Purity Plan is what has saved me from choosing to be sexual with men. There are many elements to such a plan, which I have the utmost joy in teaching people how to create. Besides extending grace, embracing self-compassion and developing self-understanding, the renewal of the mind is paramount. We need to understand ourselves, the things we say, and what is happening when we suppress our 'horny' or deny our feelings. We are communicating to ourselves that it is wrong to feel this way. How is it wrong if God has given it to us? Where did we learn that? *#selah*

Regarding the Plan, I can share with you two critical pillars: triggers and accountability. Understanding whether your trigger points are related to music, words, touch, food, hormones, etc, will transform how you embrace what you are feeling. When you know, you will be better equipped to navigate it, such as when you are ovulating, ladies, to refrain from the 'Hello, big head' text!

Accountability will save you a lot of heartache. Create the vision of who you want to be. Choose who *you* want to be, then ask trusted people to hold you to that standard. For example, my inner circle know they have permission to ask me how I am doing in this area on any day of the week, and I am obligated to tell them the truth. If they hear my thinking going left field, or they discern my heart is slightly misaligned, they will challenge me on it. They hold me accountable to who *I* said I want to be.

The characteristics you are looking for in a good accountability person include: someone who really loves you, for real; who is non-judgmental; who has sound wisdom and who will speak life to you. They also need to be someone who holds a good level of emotional intelligence and emotional stability, where making good choices is evidenced in their own lives. You will also want someone you would be afraid of letting down. Those people are worth their weight in gold.

This journey has just got a whole lot easier for you — that's if you are struggling and have chosen to implement what you've just read. I understand the journey may seem long, but I want to tell you that repentance resets the standard, and Holy Spirit is with you every step of the way.

The first step is to choose to forgive yourself. Remember, your relationship with God isn't based on performance but is grounded and rooted in unconditional love. Get busy creating a purity plan and working through your emotional baggage. Confront the darkness within. Shed the light of God on the places you may be afraid of. Become curious about why you do, think or feel the way you do. Engage in self-compassion; it will be the kindest gift you can give yourself. Accepting your sex drive and desires — and managing them *effectively* — will give you freedom, with no shame or condemnation. God gifted you with a drive and doesn't despise you because of it. Remember you have access to grace and self-control to help you through this season.

Repeat this after me: "It is perfectly OK to be single, horny and sanctified. God's grace has got me, and I have got this!"

INFORMATION ABOUT THE WRITER

Cherlene Wilson is a UK-based emotional healing coach, behaviour personality specialist, author, international speaker, and leads a ministry called Purity Talks.

Cherlene has a coaching practice that focuses on healing people's emotional wounds and helping people in the area of sexual purity, so they can uncover their most authentic, powerful and healed versions of themselves. Her superpower is her laser eye to identify emotional blockages and removing them so her clients maximise their performance and walk in the FULLNESS of their purpose and destiny.

Cherlene is also a sought-after speaker, having spoken in five continents and various media outlets, globally.

You can connect with Cherlene on Facebook and Instagram @cherlenewilson

Email: hello@cherlenewilson.co

SOMETIMES YOU HAVE TO MAKE A CHANGE

By Shermara Fletcher

There comes a point on any journey when you must assess where you are going, and whether the route you are taking is the most effective way to reach your destination. You also need the assurance that the vehicle or mode of transport is safe and dependable enough to get you there, that you are in the correct gear and, most importantly, that there is enough fuel to last the journey. In other words, you cannot expect change by doing the same things you have always done. Nothing changes if nothing changes.

On my journey of navigating singleness as a successful, educated, millennial Black woman, I realised that if I continued on the trajectory of being constantly busy, neglecting relationship-building and solely focusing on education, like many other millennials and the preceding generation, I would remain single. I needed to integrate *balance*. So, I bought myself a new vehicle, added some new sustainable fuel, changed gear and set off on a new journey. This consisted of deconstructing unhealthy social, theological and institutionally religious expectations, prioritising self-care, and showing the same intentionality to dating, relationships and love that I had shown in the other areas of my life. I also realised and accepted that God wasn't asking me to choose between my Christianity and wanting a relationship.

Now, before I continue, I am not suggesting that singleness devalues a Black Christian woman or is a consequence of not having done something 'right' or 'well enough' to become a wife. I also acknowledge that Black Christian women *do* get married, that marriage does not guarantee a happy life, and that divorce is real. There are also single Black Christian women who do not wish to be married or to have children, yet experience vibrant relationships, have amazing careers, opportunities and freedom. Quite frankly, they are living their best life!

However, this chapter is particularly speaking to single Black Christian women who *do* desire relationship and marriage, who have been waiting and are navigating the journey of disappointment as yet another birthday passes, another degree picture hangs on the wall, and another relationship prospect fails. It is also speaking to single Black Christian women who have grown up in the progressive age of feminism and are tired of being made to feel bad, that they are regressive, or are 'thirsty'. They also may be tired of upholding the superwoman lifestyle and no longer want to do it all.

I look forward to taking you on this journey.

GEAR ONE

#TheJourney

Growing up, I was that churchy pastor's kid who took part in every aspect of church — from ushering to worship leading, to running the tuck shop, to attending all-night prayer meetings, teaching Sunday school, being a youth leader, being in the comms team… and the list goes on. Any ministry and function in the church I knew, I loved, and can still perform. However, in my late teenage years to my mid-20s — when I attended university, gained post-graduate degrees and entered the young, professional working world in the bustling City of London — I started to feel unsettled.

Being churchy and working around the clock were no longer fulfilling me. I longed for relationship, my partner and a full, balanced life. I also started to notice a chilling pattern.

Many of my beautiful, professional and successful Black Christian millennial friends, who were also very churchy, were often terribly busy to the point of burnout, had over-prioritised education and church life over personal relationships, and were disproportionately single compared to friends from other ethnicities.

By my mid to late 20s, as I started to engage in more conversations, travel and speaking — through my online show, called *Beef and Justice* — I started to notice this overwhelming problem even more, and I had some overwhelming questions: Why were there so many single Black millennial and mature women in the Church? Was this a church problem or a cultural problem? Was it the men? *What was going on*?

As I started to enquire and talk to friends from the UK, the US and across the continent of Africa, I heard and could relate to echoing stories of resentment at being constantly told to wait, or to "Seek ye first the Kingdom of God and His righteousness" in response to the desire for relationship and marriage. Yes, this could work for younger women, but not when women were approaching their 30s and 40s! The frustration then grew when this verse was not being quoted for other aspects of their lives and was being repeated by loved-up couples.

As I started to have more conversations with millennials and older generations of single Black Christian women, it became clear that many of them still loved Jesus. They also still wanted to attend their church — even though their congregations were largely female, with a predominantly male leadership team and lack of male prospects in their age range. However, I noticed an increased scepticism to whether they could continue to give all their time to work and free time to church, at the expense of neglecting the time and space needed to meet their partner — especially if they wanted biological children — and saw that this strategy hadn't worked for the previous generation. There was also a sense they could potentially commit to a single life if they felt 'called' to, but were no longer willing to make that sacrifice for church-cultural causes, especially when their Christian brothers were not expected to do the same.

This really piqued my interest and, as I started to enquire about what some of the cultural reasons were, it came up repeatedly that single Black Christian women were often the workforce of the church, and did this alongside their work commitments. Whilst serving is good and builds the character of humility, pastors and spiritual leaders should also ensure, as a point of pastoral care, that their single Black female members do not become consumed in residual business, burn out or become exploited for their gifts, due to the assumption they "have more time". Also, church leaders should be sensitive in how they prioritise ministry for single people, that they do not promote a culture of 'loving your neighbour', whilst neglecting the second half of the advice which is to 'love yourself'. It's also crucial to have practical advice for single life beyond "Wait" and understand that building their personal lives will take time and sometimes take place outside of church.

Now, it can be argued that the issue of singleness within the Black female community is a wider cultural issue, following the damage of colonialism; the exploitation of the family structure which then created the strong Black woman; toxic masculinity and, ultimately, that the Church is not a dating service. This is true, and my friends and I debate this all the time, but in my conversations, the unhealthy ways in which church culture and faulty theology have also contributed to the state of Black female singleness could not be denied. Church culture *does* yield power, and influences many of the beliefs and decisions people make about their private and public lives, including building intimate relationships. This is a responsibility that cannot be taken lightly.

It was time to change gear or stay stuck.

GEAR TWO

#Myfemininity #self-love #self-carematters and #sacrificing the #StrongBlackWoman #stereotype

Another insight I discovered on my new journey was the need for prioritising femininity, rest and self-care.

This looked like creating a daily facial and beauty ritual, which consists of Elemis face balm, Nivea face cream, listening to spa meditation music on YouTube, and going to the spa every other month. I also tried the Japanese consultant, Marie Kondo's decluttering KonMari Method and committed to only keeping things in my room that spoke to my heart, and discarded items that no longer "sparked joy". This was a painful and therapeutic process, and I was surprised at how much significance the 'clutter' held for me. I would highly recommend this method because it will bring you clarity, joy and can be a key piece of preparation for how to create a peaceful environment and home in single and married life.

It is also important to take care of your styling, appearance, and knowing how to dress for your body type so that you look great, feel great and attract greatness. This may involve booking a stylist, getting your colours done, and daring yourself to wear that risky dress you don't think you can pull off. Finding time to take breaks, spending time with excellent quality friends, and creating healthy boundaries through counselling are all also important in building your femininity, self-care and self-love journey. This is not for the sole purpose of securing a relationship, but to be genuinely happy within yourself. I highly recommend that Black women unapologetically dedicate time for their self-care to ensure they have a lighter, feminine and more relaxed presence in the world.

This leads me to the number one debate my friends and I have about presence. In the world we live in, is the strong Black woman our friend or foe?

GEAR THREE

#StrongBlackWoman... #FriendorFoe?

The strong Black woman is one of the social archetypes of how Black women exist and should act in society. This has been characterised by three components: ultra-independence, emotional restraint, and taking care. This can cause Black women, including single Black Christian women, to feel pressured into becoming superwomen, to be self-sacrificial to the point of chronic stress, to have an intense drive to succeed, and to feel obligated to help others.

This is not to undermine the importance of serving or the positive influence and the many contributions and achievements Black women have acquired. However, this shouldn't come at the expense of their mental health, self-care, femininity, luxury, relationships, time to date and being open to love. It can also encourage the attitude of faithfully carrying everyone else's needs whilst neglecting their own.

One way of countering this social expectation is by tapping into femininity and mastering the art of navigating between masculine and feminine energies for different environments and relationships. Feminine traits are defined as: nurturance, sensitivity, sweetness, supportiveness, gentleness, warmth, expressiveness, modesty, humility, empathy, affection, tenderness, being emotional, kind, helpful and devoted. In contrast, masculine energy is usually defined as: strength, courage, independence, leadership, focus, competition, assertiveness, wanting to be needed and respected. Whilst it can be argued that these traits are social constructs and should not define or force women to perform to gender biases, it does also suggest that women can display external feminine beauty and still operate in masculine energy, which can repel a masculine man who is looking for his opposite in a relationship.

The purpose of highlighting the difference between masculine and feminine energy in relationships is not to discourage single Black Christian women from professional leadership roles or from being assertive; I am a keen advocate for this. Rather, it is to encourage women to resist from operating in a masculine way in all areas of their lives for their own health's sake, and especially when it comes to dating.

I evaluated this claim with a couple of my male friends and, whilst they do not represent the entire male species, their comments were interestingly similar. I asked them what they looked for when dating and what led to a successful relationship. Whilst they were proud and supported the amazing advancements of their partner, they repeatedly mentioned that this was not the key to their initial attraction. They mentioned her femininity, softness, how she took care of herself, that she was fun to be around, had clear standards and boundaries, and gave them a sense of peace.

There are countless femininity tutorials on YouTube for Black women, teaching about the art of femininity for self-care and relationships. Many also encourage Black women to resist carrying the weight and responsibility of civic, community and financial life all on their own.

One YouTuber I listen to is Dr Michelle Daf. You can check out one of her videos if you type in this link https://bit.ly/MichDef

GEAR FOUR

#The #journey of #intentionality

As I mentioned at the beginning of this chapter, I had to make some changes to my journey to position myself for my desired destination. Intentionality was a key part of this. The story of Ruth and Boaz shows that intentionally positioning oneself in safe spaces where men are — and not waiting on the sidelines to picked — is an effective dating technique.

Just like Ruth was intentional about being seen by Boaz in his space, single Black Christian women — who want to be married and for whom there is a lack of men in their churches — should be likewise encouraged to spend more time in other spaces where the men *will* be. This can be done by expanding their hobbies, joining clubs and the gym, sports centres, attending networking events, salsa classes, coffee shops and even the car wash. Safely trying online dating may also be a choice. I say 'safely' because there are some real horror stories, but there have been some great relationship outcomes too. It could also be time to fix that broken item in your house and visit the hardware store… A single man may be able to help you find what you are looking for!

There are also traditional matchmaking services that single Black Christian women can tap into, where relationship coaches and experts can help you to find your match. This may require tearing up that list and being open to the new possibilities.

Now, there is also the reality of single Black Christian women who are being intentional and venturing into the dating minefield — or the 'jungle', as it is called these days — and are still not finding success. I believe there needs to be a robust pastoral care strategy for this, as they are still single, it still hurts, and the last thing they want to hear is a flippant "Wait on the Lord". What if we saw Black women's singleness as a heavy burden we *all* must carry? How might our ethical approach to this dilemma change *then*?

GEAR 5
#Continuing #thejourney

So, as I continue to change gears, fill up the fuel in my new vehicle and enjoy this new journey, I hope you will too. I hope this journey helps you move gear and comforts you in knowing that you are not alone. I also hope you find the tools to resist gaslighting against your desire for a relationship, and that you will not be silenced, made to feel guilty, desperate or invalidated for wanting the beauty of a relationship manifested through the commitment of marriage.

And remember, relationships and marriage are not only a good idea, but they are also a *God* idea, so do not give up on your journey

INFORMATION ABOUT THE WRITER

Shermara Fletcher is an international speaker, influencer, singer and writer. Professionally, Shermara is committed to ensuring that the Church is represented well in public life and has done extensive work in the area of homelessness. She is the youngest woman to be appointed to the national role of Principal Officer for Pentecostal, Charismatic and Multi-Cultural Relations at Churches Together in England (CTE). Shermara keeps it real and has a passion for inspiring and empowering women to be their best selves. She has worked within women's ministry under her mother, Rev Joyce Fletcher, for over 10 years and loves to see women shine.

You can connect with Shermara at www.facebook.com/shermara.fletcher.5

Email: shermarafletcher_1@outlook.com

THE DIGITAL SEARCH FOR LOVE

by Andrina Davis

5′ 8", non-smoker, laid-back, with a great sense of humour...

I looked at the picture again. It said anything *but* 'laid-back with a great sense of humour'. It actually looked like a person who was very intense and who got angry regularly... But how much can you tell from a picture?

I sighed. Internet dating had become the bane of my life. It felt like a catch 22: a laborious and arduous way to meet someone, but with my lifestyle and current prospects, possibly the *only* way I would meet someone halfway decent.

I am one of those people old enough to remember the days before the Internet and before internet dating — the 'good old days' — where we had to meet people naturally, organically and in person. I'm really showing my age now, but I remember when dating sites first became a '*thing*'. In the early stages, they were still treated with scepticism and mistrust by most of the population. Meeting someone off the 'murky, dark place called the Internet' was seen as dangerous, and only for *desperate* people who couldn't meet anyone in the 'normal' way.

"She meets men off the Internet" was mockingly whispered under hushed tones, by married people who were fortunate enough to have met their partners IRL (in real life), and by some single people who swore they would *never* degrade themselves by turning to the Internet.

I smiled ironically at how times have changed. Apparently, around 39% of relationships begin online nowadays. (I have to admit I thought it would have been higher.) It is suspected, however, that if current trends continue, more people will meet their partners online than offline by 2035.

Of course, you still have the staunch singletons who refuse to engage in online dating. My good friend is one of them. As a single Christian woman in her 60s, she would *never* turn to the Internet to find a potential partner. No matter how much I've tried to encourage her to give it a try, I am always met with the retort, "It's just not for me."

I looked back at the profile in front of me. I didn't think internet dating was '*for me*' either. However, I appeared to have got myself into a place where it felt like my only realistic prospect of meeting someone in this day and age, especially if I wanted to meet a Christian man.

Like many of my single Christian sisters in their 20s and 30s, the prospect of meeting a single Christian man in his 30s at church or in my community is slim to none. The odds go down further if I want to meet a man who is actually interested in me. The competition out there is fierce, and whenever I look at my gorgeous, successful single female Christian friends, I often think, 'What hope do *I* have?'

Don't get me wrong. Aside from being a little overweight, I'm not ugly, and when I make an effort... I scrub up really well! The problem is, I haven't been making much of an effort recently… and life, work, church and single motherhood have been getting in the way. Those were further reasons I felt it was less likely for me to meet someone "organically".

Online, I could put my best foot forward. My pictures could be a 'fresh Andrina', relaxing on holiday, kissed by the sun and without a care in the world. It would definitely not be the day-to-day Andrina the world saw. I hoped this would be enough to grab the attention of a great Christian man, who would be willing to give me a chance.

My mind drifted back to the profile in front of me. I had been swiping for a while now. Searching through online dating profiles can become mind-numbing. You learn very quickly how to disregard matches by skimming a profile for a few seconds: sexually explicit language, unflattering pictures, kissing his dog on the lips… these are all pretty easy ways to prompt you to move on! You can spend seconds on a profile before discounting them, always in the hope that the next profile will be better. That can also become a problem with internet dating. It gives you the false assurance that someone better is always round the corner. Swiping can become addictive, like the high of continuously placing a bet in the hopes you'll win something big the next time round. When we had less choice, our expectations were not as high, and we probably would have settled for less. But, when you're given the false impression that there is an abundance, you become picky...

The guy in front of me did not mention 'Christian' anywhere on his profile. I had learnt to become quite open to different types of people, and tried not to discount them too easily, but this was one of my must-haves... Well, it *generally* was, unless the guy was really REALLY good looking. (Don't judge me — haven't you ever heard of 'missionary dating'?)

Nowadays, most guys seemed to have 'Christian' set as the default on their profile, but there was nothing to indicate they were practising or committed Christians. I reminded myself I was not currently on a Christian dating site, but one of the free social media dating sites, although I'm sure I had profiles on every dating site going — Christian *and* secular. I wanted to give myself the best possible chance and cast my net far and wide... You never know where my future husband could be hiding. But this guy was definitely not him. I clicked the "X" and moved on to the next profile.

And that was it. This is what my dating life had become. Mindlessly swiping online, whilst *Coronation Street* played in the background.

I suspect a lot of single Christians can sympathise with my predicament, especially those who have been single for a while. Sometimes it feels like, at its best, it can be disheartening and, at its worse, it can be downright depressing.

I met someone recently who had everything I had been looking for. After months of mindless swiping, a good-looking Christian man appeared on my screen, and I allowed myself to become hopeful. I was hesitant at first, as this man had a lot of baggage — another dilemma single people face. As we get older, the people we meet will come with more baggage (we will too). So, I was reluctant, but I allowed myself to be swept away by this man, and convinced myself we could overcome and manage the baggage we both brought to the relationship.

As the relationship progressed, on the outside, he looked like the perfect man – my family and friends all liked him — and I suspect some of my single friends may have even experienced a hint of jealousy that I appeared to have found someone so "perfect". I painfully admit I would have probably had similar feelings if the shoe were on the other foot.

However, the cracks in the relationship soon began to show, and I realised that there's a significant difference between someone's personality and their character. The personality is what people see: the laughing, fun, helpful person. However, a person's *character* speaks to their integrity, their self-control, their trustworthiness and their honesty — or lack thereof…

There were a number of instances during our relationship where this man engaged in behaviours that demonstrated his true character. They were behaviours I could not even talk to my friends about, as they would have asked me why I remained in the relationship. If I were counselling someone, and they shared that their partner had behaved in some of the same ways, I would have queried why they remained in the relationship too, and I would have likely questioned their feelings of self-worth and self-esteem. However, being on the receiving end of these behaviours, and feeling like I was in love with this man, I convinced myself that no-one was perfect, and I had to compromise if I wanted to get married. I also admit I didn't want people to think I couldn't maintain a relationship, no matter how badly I was being treated.

This is where I learned another dating tip: there is a difference between 'compromise' and 'settling'.

Compromise is choosing to be flexible and accepting behaviours or traits you wouldn't normally want to, all because the other aspects of the person and relationship fulfil you. However, when you settle, you compromise on your needs. You make do with less, because you believe this is the best you can do (maybe because of your age, your looks or your personality). You tell yourself you have to accept whatever you're given if you ever want to be married. However, when you settle, you risk your long-term happiness and contentment.

I have always prided myself on not settling for less than I deserved. However, there were times when I asked whether I should have just settled so that I could be married. I recognise that my standards had likely been too high in the past, however, now I worry my standards are too low, and that I will accept anyone out of sheer desperation to be married. Thankfully, I know this is not true, as I am no longer in the relationship I knew I should not have been in. Don't get me wrong, break-ups are hard, and I am still nursing a broken heart. Sometimes, even when your head knows it's for the best, you still have a hard time convincing your heart.

I can move forward, as I am certain God will reward me for my faithfulness. I knew this relationship was not God's will or God's best for me, and as difficult as it was, I chose to honour God with my body and mind, rather than remain in a relationship that likely would have destroyed me and my relationship with God. I trust I will have the relationship God desires for me, and I will not accept counterfeits or substitutes. I desire to have a relationship that honours God, and I know God wants this for me also.

As I look back at the Church's response to the 'singleness crisis', I recognise they have not always got things right. I believe there came a season when there was a shift in how people met and got married. The Church did not keep up with this shift and was left behind whilst the world moved on. The Church then ended up in an awkward position, where it was trying to encourage marriages, but didn't know how to.

I have often found myself frustrated at the way the Church (church leadership in particular) has catered for and ministered to single people. However, I came to the realisation that it wasn't due to a lack of desire to help, but rather due to not really knowing *how* to help.

I am a woman of action, so I have supported a number of church initiatives over the past few years in an attempt to assist the church in ministering to single people, as well as ensuring that single people are visible and heard. One of the most powerful events I have held recently was a workshop entitled 'Has the Church failed single people?" This was initially supposed to be a presentation to the senior leadership of my church. However, I felt God had a bigger purpose for it, so I made it a public event (ensuring that the leadership of my church would be in attendance). Through facilitating this event, I discovered there was a real need for healing and restoration of single people. It became apparent that some single people blame the Church for keeping them single, and are experiencing bitterness and sadness about the life they feel they have missed out on.

I would encourage every person, who has a heart for single people, to ensure that the single people in their lives and congregations have an outlet to express their true feelings around their singleness, and that they are supported in their healing and restoration. Not every person who desires to be married will get married, so the Church and church community have a responsibility to support those who may be struggling with this realisation.

Before I go, I would like to leave you with a few tips I have picked up in my years of dating:

- Whether you choose to venture into the world of online dating or opt for a more organic way of meeting people, be positive! As mundane, frustrating and disappointing as things may be, you should always be positive and believe the process will yield results. Try visualising success. In your mind, see yourself meeting someone amazing and have that expectation.
- Date to gather data, not to get married. As controversial as this may seem, I always recommend people go out on as many dates as they can. Even if someone does not seem like your type, go out with them. Going for a coffee is not accepting a marriage proposal! How will you know whether they are marriage material if you don't give them a chance?

The ultimate aim for most singletons is to get married, but there are a lot of steps we must take before we get there.

- This is likely going to prove unpopular, but we have to understand that as we get older, we will likely have to lower our expectations. The dating pool significantly reduces as we get older, and there are some things we may need to be more open to that we would not have been if we were younger. You may have never wanted to date someone who has been divorced, or who has children, but these may need to be requirements you reconsider as you get older, if you would like to get married.
- Guard your heart. Speaking from personal experience, it is very easy to fall in love quickly when you meet someone who appears to have most of the qualities you're looking for. However, it's likely you will be experiencing the 'honeymoon' phase of the relationship, and it will take three to six months to really get to know someone and their character. I don't advise you to put barriers up, but I *do* advise that you remain mindful that there will still be a lot about this person you don't know, and only time will reveal their true characteristics. Have fun getting to know them, but continue to evaluate them and their character.
- Work on yourself. I was recently reminded by a male friend that men (Christian men included) are visual beings, and they are attracted by what they see. Try to work on your physical health, lose the weight if you can, and become more toned. We also have to work on our characters and personalities. Some of us have become so jaded by life and love, we are miserable to be around. Your future partner will want to meet someone fun, who has a thirst and excitement for life. I always recommend that singletons get counselling to help them process some of the trauma and hardships they've been through, so they don't take them into relationships.

- Cover your dating life with prayer. It may seem like this should not even need to be mentioned, but I question how many singletons are really seeking God in this area of their lives. I am also a big advocate for prayer and fasting in this area, and for calling a group of people to pray consistently for this. We have to have faith that God cares about us and every aspect of our lives, including our desire for a partner. He will sustain us, as long as we remain in His will.

God bless you all!

Dear God

I thank You that You care about even the littlest things in our lives. Thank You for being beside us during our darkest and loneliest times. You know our desires and the pain we can sometimes feel as we wait on You. I pray that You sustain each of us during this period of waiting. I pray that You bring the right people into our lives. I pray against counterfeits, substitutes and distractions. Thank You that Your strength is made perfect in our weakness, as there are many times we feel weak along this journey. I pray that You satisfy the deepest longings of our hearts with Your intimate presence. Answer our prayers in the way You see fit, Lord, and help us to be content with Your answer. We love You, Lord, and desire to please You on this journey. Be with us, in Jesus' Name. Amen.

INFORMATION ABOUT THE WRITER

Andrina is a single mum from Birmingham, UK, and is the founder of Divine Introductions, an agency that creates opportunities for single Christians to meet and connect.

Andrina is active within her local church, and serves on the Worship Team, the IT/Audio Visual Team and in Public Relations.

She is passionate about seeing women succeed in all aspects of their lives and has a special proclivity towards single Christian women. Her desire is to see women thrive and grow in whatever circumstances they find themselves in.

Connect with Andrina at www.facebook.com/DivineIntroductions/

Email: andrinadavis@hotmail.co.uk

THE WAY WE WERE

by Theresa Beckles

In 1992 I became a Christian at the age of 35. My coming to Christ occurred after a miraculous healing I'd experienced from God, and that was when I decided I had to find not just a church but my Healer — Jesus Christ — again.

I had met a wonderful young man three years earlier, and we had talked about marriage, but whilst doing my research in studying the Bible I came across this Scripture in Matthew 19:9,

> *"And I say unto you whoever divorces his wife except for sexual immorality and marries another commits adultery, and whoever marries her who is divorced commits adultery."*

I felt heavily convicted by this verse, so I decided to seek advice. I needed a full explanation, because I was a divorcee and wanted to get married again.

I was advised to get baptised first, then see whether marriage was what the Holy Ghost wanted me to pursue.

During my early walk with Christ, I didn't notice any of the women's attitudes towards singleness at first, as I was heavily involved in ministry. What I *did* notice, however, was that no one asked me about the young man I had first walked into church with. Unbeknown to them, he lived abroad, and was only in the UK on vacation. To my horror, I discovered some years later that there had been notes held on me, saying I needed to be watched as I had a boyfriend! And, to add insult to injury, I was refused baptism as it was assumed we were living together IN SIN!!!

If only they knew what that poor man had to go through while he was here… He believed I had to be seeing someone else, as there had been no hanky panky coming from me, such was my heavy conviction from reading the Word. Thank God for Jesus — the all-seeing, omnipresent, omniscient, omnipotent God.

The church I attended consisted of an equal amount of both young male and female singletons. There were only a few marriages taking place during those early days, and the church was on hand to assist the couple on the wedding day with the arrangements. It was a strange time, as very few people in the congregation would have been aware that a couple were even courting, until the day when there was a surprise announcement of their engagement!

The married women at the time seemed distant from the singles; there weren't many interactions between them. To be honest, half the time it was difficult to know who was married to whom, as married couples didn't have a lot of interactions with each other — let alone any PDAs (public displays of affection).

Bearing in mind this was in the early 90s, I recall a sister crying after one such engagement announcement, saying it "should have been her", as she had been in church working in ministry with this brother, and couldn't understand why he had chosen to marry someone else. I got the impression there was no such thing as dating, so looking back on some of the failed marriages I can now understand why dating didn't work! Having had conversations years later with some of the people whose marriages had failed, they confessed there had been no such thing as dating alone. They had got to know each other mainly through telephone conversations, which also came with a warning that no-one should call anyone of the opposite sex after 9pm! Neither could they be seen by themselves on a date without a chaperone. If they dated, it was all done in secret!

The preaching from the pulpit at the time also seemed to concentrate on Fornication!!! Fornication!!! Fornication!!! As if that were the only form of sin! Thank God for the Word that kept us singletons sane: 'The acts of the flesh are obvious: sexual immorality, impurity and debauchery; idolatry and witchcraft; hatred; discord, jealousy, fits of rage, selfish ambition, dissensions, factions and envy; drunkenness, orgies and the like. I warn you, as I did before, that those who live like this will not inherit the Kingdom of God' (Galatians 5:19-21).

As much as fornication was preached, there was no balance regarding marriage. There was no encouragement or teaching towards marriage. Furthermore, judging by how the married couples interacted — or rather seeing the lack of interactions between husband and wife — there was nothing to aspire to. It didn't make me feel as though I was missing out on anything. However, this might be because I had been there before, bought the t-shirt and had worn it well.

One of the brothers in later years said of that time he felt like it was a curse being single, as though only single people committed sin. In those days, if you were seen merely *talking* to a member of the opposite sex as a singleton, you were watched. Big Brother was in operation, lol. I often wondered how on earth did some of these married couples ever get together! Then I found out…

Another brother confessed that as he and a young woman were the only two single people in their church at the time, they were 'TOLD': "You two need to get married" and that was the end of that! Sadly, one of the married sisters said the same thing, and later learned that her husband refused to commit to the marriage because he confessed he wanted to marry another sister in the church. Unfortunately, she had married someone else.

All this hurt and pain that my brothers and sisters went through is hard to swallow. I wonder what God has to say about all these failings that have been laden upon them due to the misunderstanding of their leaders.

Others who came to church as co-habiting couples were told to get married or end their relationship!

Some got married out of pure lust…. hence the marriage failed.

1 Corinthians 7:9 reads: 'Now to the unmarried and widows I say it is good for them to stay unmarried, as I do. But if they cannot control themselves, they should marry, for it is better to marry than to burn with passion.' As for me and my house, I would rather choose to burn, lol, because divorce, moving house and bereavement are not easy!

Some of the brothers found out to their detriment that marriage was not all it was cracked up to be, as their wives continued to live as singletons rather than as wives — some refusing to cook or even do basic housework. They had married a trophy wife! They had gone for the hair, the light skin colour and the looks, completely ignoring Proverbs 18:22 – 'He who finds a wife finds a good thing and obtains favour from the Lord.'

I remember one wise woman saying: "A ring does not make you a wife." How true. It seems it was all about the ring as a status symbol and not the marriage.

I myself was once called into a meeting and told that a certain brother had asked for my hand in marriage. Having only just become a new believer and having gone through the motions of being told/advised that I should wait on the Lord and see what He says, I was speechless.

As the years went by, and the church became more relaxed about people letting God be the One to convict them in how they dress/act, etc, I noticed that some of the women started to behave in such an unnatural way towards the brothers. They looked uncomfortable and behaved uncomfortably. Some even confided in me that God had told them a particular brother was going to be their husband. Unfortunately for them I already knew that the brother in question was on the verge of becoming engaged to someone else!

I asked one sister why she thought a particular brother was going to be her husband and was shocked to hear that his only conversation with her had been: "Sis, I like your new hairstyle." Sadly, in her dreams, she thought that was all it took to get married, even talking about how many children they would have and what they would look like! This is the result of all the restrictions that were put upon us women during those times. No wonder the Bible says in Luke 16:8 that 'the children of this world are, in their own generation, wiser than the children of light.'

I have always been used to being around men. From an early age, my older brother had many friends who would come over to our house during the school holidays. He made sure, however, to warn them that if any of them thought or even *looked* at his sister, they'd be dead.

My career choice also found me working predominantly with men, and as such, many of my friends were mostly men. What seemed to me to be a natural way of life — to be able to just be yourself and be confident amongst men — I realised it wasn't so for many of the women in church, especially those who were brought up in church. What a mess! The Big Brother tactics of the church had turned the women into adopting what the world would call frigid, weird, unnatural and uncomfortable behaviour.

I guess my confidence in speaking and listening to anyone made it easier for others to confide in me, whether it was in church or at work.

Divorce was also a hot topic to be shunned. It was said that if a person met a divorced woman, they had better find out the reason for her divorce. Divorcees were not allowed to work in what was known as primary ministry, i.e. altar call, choir, etc.

As a divorcee, however, I managed to escape that one, as I became involved in ministry work the very day I emerged from the waters of baptism. To be honest, most people today have only just learnt I was married prior to being saved.

Fast forward to today, and the Church is much more relaxed about divorce. Many who taught strongly on the topic in days gone by have themselves gotten divorced and have remarried. Some, even for a second and third time!!!

I was fortunate to be chosen to help plan and execute several of the weddings that took place at my former churches, and served as a shoulder to cry on for those who had lost loved ones through death.

Unfortunately, life for the older single woman hasn't changed much. So many, who have been brought up in church and spent all their lives doing the will of God, are still unmarried. They are the Church's 'hidden secret' — Pentecostal virgins — to be returned unopened.... How sad.

Many have given their lives to the work and cause of the ministry, only to be told "Just pray" if they ever muster up the courage to mention the hope of becoming a wife and mother. I feel many of my sisters wouldn't have been single had they not received bad teaching and counselling.

We were encouraged to marry a Christian man…. or, should I say, "a *Pentecostal* Christian man", as spouses had to come from the same denomination, as 'just Christian' wasn't good enough.

I understand why churches had this stance, however, if we look around the churches today, the ratio of men to women is almost 1 to 50!!! OK, I'm exaggerating a little, but the male/female ratio is heavily weighted in men's favour! To add to that misery there is the imbalance of work, church, work and, over the years, many of the churches now function as an island. They don't hold as many conventions (major church events held over several days), which provide opportunities to meet other people from different churches and form friendships.

Due to the male/female imbalance in the Church, and difficulty in finding partners, some women have become hardened, and unfortunately you can see the stress and strain on their faces. Others are in denial: "I don't need a husband; it's just me and God. We're good…"

It is heartbreaking to see and hear my sisters crying, feeling they haven't even had the opportunity to do nor accomplish what women of other cultures throughout the world have: simply being a wife and mother. I know the Bible says to "pick up your cross and follow Me" (Matthew 16:24-26), but what a cross to bear…

Sadly, I remember losing a dear Christian sister who died of a broken heart. Literally!

I had learnt, too late, that she had been admitted to hospital and had discharged herself several times. Why? She had become an alcoholic and had hidden this fact for a long time. She always had a smile on her face and would always change the subject back to you whenever she was asked: "How are you?" She would say: "God is good." As Christians, we all know that He IS good, however, that answer always makes me turn around and say: "Yes, I know, but how are YOU?"

She eventually confided in me that she had been seeing someone for some time, and wanted him to marry her, but he said he wasn't ready. Unfortunately, she found out within months of him saying he "wasn't ready" that he got married to someone else! Sadly that must have been the start of her demise; she drank herself to death.

When she was admitted to hospital, her liver was in such a state it was beyond repair. I'm still broken and don't think I can ever get over such an untimely death. Sad that someone amongst us could end this way. I've learnt that we mustn't be fooled by the fake smile, when deep down people are wearing a mask and are in denial.

My message to every single person out there is: do not hide behind a mask. Speak your truth. We *are* our brother's keeper.

Do not forsake the fellowship of others; do not do lip service; spend time getting to know one another. Jesus Himself had close friendships with His disciples. How can we say we are saved if we don't build relationships with each other? There's a saying which states 'Charity begins at home' so let's begin to recognise our own, those who are in front of us, before we look further afield to others.

And, as for the young single women, do not be afraid to speak your truth. Marriage is ordained by God, and if it is your desire to be wed, then speak it out and prepare for it. The same way you prepare for a job or look after your car, do the same for marriage. Check your motives and character; understand the meaning of marriage; communicate, do your due diligence; do not limit yourself; do not make a long list; make sure your partner shares the same values as you. Speak to the older women. Don't make the same mistakes we did. And be wise.

'Where there is no guidance, a people falls, but in an abundance of counsellors there is safety' (Proverbs 11:14).

INFORMATION ABOUT THE WRITER

Theresa Beckles has been a Christian for over three decades and has served in church administrative and leadership teams. Theresa also runs an event and wedding planning business, does room decoration and flower arranging and is renowned for her caring and compassionate nature.

You can connect with Theresa at www.instagram.com/exclusivelyyouevents/

Email: info@exclusivelyyouevents.co.uk

SINGLENESS, HEALING AND WHOLENESS

by Belinda Smith

Singleness is not a curse, and it isn't something that needs 'fixing'.

In my day job as a psychotherapist, I work with a lot of women in the Church who unfortunately treat singleness as though it is a curse. Some say they can be made to feel like they are cursed. Truth be told, sometimes it can feel as if it is.

Being single can take women to the land of *"I'm not good enough. What's wrong with me? Am I too loud? Am I ugly? Am I too tall or too short? Did I talk too much when I met him or too little? Do I need to be sexier and flirt more?"* And being in this space can be exhausting and painful, because singleness leaves women coping with feelings of sadness, depression, loss or grief over what they are missing out on, and disappointment, guilt or anger. These emotions can have a negative impact on anyone's self-esteem and confidence.

It is easy for a single woman to look on women who are in relationships and ask themselves the question: 'What does *she* have that I don't?' or 'She must have what guys are looking for and I clearly don't have whatever it is that guys want in a woman/wife.'

A false narrative that women have been taught over time is that good things come to those who deserve them and wait. The danger, however, is that those who aren't in a relationship can feel they aren't deserving of love, companionship or real happiness. The waiting is exhausting and, subconsciously, single Christians have unknowingly cancelled themselves or have used their past to sabotage their future rather than use their past to inform it.

A woman's head may be saying 'I want a husband', but her heart is telling her she won't ever have one and, as a result, this impacts on how she positions herself as a single woman in the world.

Traditionally, there have always been more women in our churches than men, so that in itself has been a challenge. I have counselled many Black Christian women, who heard and received the preached message: "Be faithful in serving the Lord in His house and your husband will find you." So, they did just that! They served, waited and waited, and maybe didn't do anything else. Now they experience life, feeling like the gift of marriage and children has passed them by. Today these women (including you, maybe?) have unwittingly and inadvertently become invisible due to a lot of the teachings in our churches. Those noteworthy doctrines over the years made women dress in unflattering clothes, and the teachings made many feel less attractive and less approachable. Some of these women are now dealing with a lot of shame and secretly putting themselves down for being single.

Some women listen to the voices in their head telling them everything they did wrong is why they are still single. It's important they have a safe space to talk about how they feel and to acknowledge the sadness and the pain. These feelings are real. What is also real is the conflict of women wanting a life partner but then not wanting to be seen as though they 'need' a man. Being single can be fulfilling but so can being in a relationship.

RELATIONSHIP COUNSELLING

I work with many female clients who come to see me for relationship counselling, even when they are single. By working with a counsellor, these women understand I can support and help them to develop a better relationship with themselves. The most crucial relationship anyone needs to have in life, first and foremost, is always going to be the relationship they have with themselves.

Professional experience has taught me that one of the main issues arising from the therapeutic work I do with single women, including Christian women, is centred around the relationship women have with themselves.

If a woman doesn't know herself, let alone know how to be honest and kind to herself, can she really expect to have a good relationship with someone else? Counselling helps women to take responsibility of their own feelings, thoughts and actions. It also assists them in working on their personal boundaries and becoming more aware of what they like, what they want and more so what they need.

Being single doesn't define a person, and it's important we don't view singleness as something to be 'fixed'. It's what a person is at a particular moment in time, and it's a status that is subject to change.

It's easy for women to think they have done something wrong and it's their fault why they are single — especially in a society that tells us we can't be complete without a partner. God hasn't abandoned ladies who are single. A single person is absolutely just as good enough and there is nothing 'wrong' with them. They are not unlovable or dysfunctional because this one desire of their heart has currently been left untouched by God. But there are things an individual can start and work on to benefit themselves.

THE BENEFIT OF THERAPY

Unfortunately, Christian women can, at times, lack intentionality in the area of finding love. The desire is there but teaching in this area has led to the assumption that it will just happen! However, nothing 'just happens'.

Black Christian women, in particular, have been instructed to be passive in the search for love. So sadly, they feel they have been left with nothing, because they have been taught to do 'nothing', other than pray and be overly dogmatic about the type of man they should want. It is imperative that godly Black men and women, rather than blaming the Church, place their focus on changing this scenario, especially for the next generation. We still also have to trust and believe that if someone desires to get married, it can happen whether they are 20 or 50.

I know this to be true because I have worked with women who have gone from being single to getting married after working on their core beliefs; exploring their thoughts and feelings about relationships, and by taking a look at their past and present relationships.

These clients learned the importance of examining how they interact with others; how they communicate their feelings, and how they develop their relationships. All these factors play a part in how someone 'shows up' in the world.

I tell women they must delve into and understand why they may be drawn to people who disappoint or devalue them. My work with single women has increased not just their confidence and communication skills but also their ability to *see themselves* before expecting that man to see them. They therefore develop a stronger sense of 'self'. Healthy people are attractive and are increasingly more likely to attract healthy people.

CASE STUDY

Kate*, 56, Christian and single, is one woman I did some therapeutic work with. When I started working with her, we initially focused on the impact her traumatic upbringing was having on her and also the impact her singleness was having on her view of herself, people and the world. She carried an emotional and mental burden as a result of thinking that something was wrong with her because she had been single for so long. Kate felt unlovable and dysfunctional because that one desire of her heart — to find love and be married — had been left unmet by God. I worked with Kate to reframe her story, and we also worked on her inner child which empowered her to trust herself. She was then able to apply that strong mind and desire given by God to happily pursue her goals and God-given assignments. Previously her strong mind and desire had motivated her in every other area of her life except in the area of love. In that area, she had played at being demure and had sat pretty on the sidelines, waiting to be picked.

We did intense work that changed her perspective and attitude towards herself and her desire to be married. Kate put some legs on that desire, and went to a friend's anniversary dinner where she met a man who 'appeared' not to be her type. Suspending her inner child fears a little, she exchanged numbers with him in February 2020, and married the same man in April 2021. She continued her work with me every single week throughout lockdown to address her fears, anxiety issues and past pain, whilst allowing this man to love on her which she was far from accustomed to.

DOING THE WORK

Therapeutic work is necessary because it allows single women the chance to look at their attachment styles and therefore the ways they perceive and respond to intimacy in romantic relationships. As adults we have three attachment styles that we developed as children as a product of our upbringing, but we are also influenced by a variety of factors including our life experiences.

Secure women tend to feel comfortable with intimacy and they are usually warm and loving. ***Anxious*** women crave intimacy but tend to worry about whether their partners love them back. ***Avoidant*** women equate intimacy with the loss of their independence, so they continuously diminish closeness.

These attachment styles impact on how an individual:

- views intimacy and togetherness
- deals with conflict
- communicates feelings, thoughts, wishes and needs

It also impacts their attitude towards sex, and their expectations of a partner and the relationship.

Although most women want to be in a relationship, I have come to realise many don't realise that their attachment styles and wounds don't actually allow them to. These styles don't allow them to be present, seen, heard, loved, trusting, confident, deserving, kind to themselves, expressive, forgiving, compromising, aware, self-reflecting, vulnerable, feminine, wanting, dependent, open, comfortable, genuine or remotely honest.

Some women and, it has to be said, men too are literally keeping love at arm's length and don't even know it.

SINGLE AND FEARFUL

Being single can be lonely and learning to cope with this loneliness can be very difficult. Although it isn't as stigmatised today as it was in the past, it doesn't take away the very real, raw emotions that can accompany being single. What can make this process most painful is the very real feeling that 'being single will never end'. Uncertainty feeds anxiety and breeds fear.

A lot of single women live in fear, a fear that keeps them living in the past, while others just can't wait to be propelled into the future. Being present in the moment is where we can discover true acceptance and contentment. Living in the past or in the ideal future brings no peace. So the question here is, what is causing the fear?

Leading with fear will cause an individual to emotionally fight, flight, freeze or fawn. All these responses play a part in how someone navigates through the dating world and through the world as a whole.

In reality, many single women are moving through life as frightened, hurting, confused, broken, lost girls. Their inner child has taken the wheel of their life and is making all their major decisions. The fear of being rejected or abandoned causes them to shut down or sabotage relationships. The need for approval from others causes them to make unhealthy choices, and because self-worth is tied to putting others first, fear of saying 'No' informs the boundaries a woman might set for herself. The need to be rescued or saved can also hinder her healing journey.

Many single women are still carrying wounds obtained through mistreatment by parents, partners and church leaders. Those wounds changed how some women saw themselves; how they felt people saw them and, in the process, changed core beliefs. Some women believe they are single because they are not worthy or deserving of safe and secure relationships. It's important that women who feel this way make choices that make them feel safe and happy. They may even need to learn to be more assertive and intentional as a single woman.

Inner child work entails dealing with the wounds of old that are very much present today. For instance, the **Wound of Abandonment** can leave someone with the fear of being left or being alone, and usually results in a woman being attracted to emotionally unavailable men.

The **Guilt Wound** is afraid to set boundaries and doesn't like to ask for things. It usually results in women attracting men who will make them feel guilty.

The **Trust Wound** leaves women feeling afraid of being hurt, finds ways not to trust people and results in attracting men who don't make a woman feel safe or secure.

The **Neglect Wound** leaves individuals with low self-worth, repressed emotions and fear of being vulnerable. This Wound normally results in attracting men who don't appreciate women or make them feel unseen.

A lot of relationship issues can be linked to not addressing inner child wounds.

No matter what the wound is, a wounded person will subconsciously pick partners they believe can heal that wound, but usually end up getting a person of the exact opposite who ends up exacerbating the very same wounds. The great thing is, however, those wounds can be healed with counselling, therapy, self-help and self-love.

THE PATH TO HEALING

Any woman desiring love must position themselves properly, so they can move from singleness to marriage and occupy a space in the world that allows them to be seen for who they really are. I'm speaking of moving from being broken to being whole. I'm NOT speaking about *becoming* anyone but *un*becoming someone! I'm talking about doing the work to unlearn the toxic and unhealthy patterns, behaviours and beliefs and the general ways of being that individuals were forced to become or learnt to survive their experiences — whether at home, school, work, church, etc.

It's about regaining a true sense of self because singleness has a way of redefining identity. Being single in the Black Church today can be stressful and, for some, traumatic. When you realise and reflect on the fact that your present self is being impacted by being single, only then can you begin the process of unlearning, relearning and soothing your inner self, so that you are able to show up as your true self and be really seen.

The significance of being Christian and single must be explored. For some it isn't only about not having a partner; it can also be about not having a family or children. It's about dealing with the loss of not being a wife, a mother, a grandmother or even a great-grandmother. For some, they are having to sit in the pain of deep disappointment and having to learn to accept what can feel is unacceptable. For others, it's an opportunity to fill their own self-love tank.

Although difficult, it's important you don't fall into the self-loathing hole when you're single. Time alone can also afford us the real time to find ourselves, find our purpose and really discover our passion. It is vital to know that married people are not necessarily happier than single people.

Moving forward, Christian women need to commit to reversing the dire statistics around marriage in our community. It's OK to be intentional about finding a spouse, which might mean going to therapy as well as going to that special event, broadening your social circle or going online.

Be relaxed about it, and then allow God to do the rest.

*(*Name changed to protect identity)*

INFORMATION ABOUT THE WRITER

Belinda Smith is a qualified counsellor, psychotherapist and founder of The Yakira Centre (TYC) that provides an affordable counselling and therapeutic service. TYC also teaches accredited counselling courses. A former youth leader, Belinda has many years of experience providing counselling and therapy for individuals, couples and families who have various issues including mental health problems, relationships difficulties and anxiety.

Connect with Belinda at www.theyakiracentre.com

Email: info@theyakiracentre.com

FINDING A GOOD CHRISTIAN WOMAN

by A A Jones

Since the global ratio of women is higher than that of men, a lot of people assume men would have an easy time finding the 'woman of their dreams'. This assumption is far from the truth for many men, however — including some Christian men. There are myriads of reasons why numerous men struggle to find the woman of their dreams, and these reasons vary from man to man.

Many Christian men desire to marry 'a good Christian woman', and our churches are seemingly filled with women who fit that description. The question is, however, why are there so many good Christian women out there, expecting to be found, while a lot of Christian men are complaining that it's hard to find one?

After touring different cities and countries with our Connect Conferences, and after counselling countless men over the years, it's clear that finding a good Christian woman to marry is considered by several men to be a complex task.

Our churches are filled with amazing single women, most of whom know how to pray, fast, seek the face of the Lord, live a holy life, run a successful business, have a successful career and work very hard. As good as these qualities are, it takes more than these to be a good wife, and many Christian men want to see other important qualities in the women they hope to spend the rest of their lives with.

The dilemma, however, is that the extra qualities many Christian men desire to find in a Christian woman are not often emphasised in churches, neither is it a subject most men can comfortably talk about without being judged. This is why you will see some Christian men attending a church full of Christian women, yet *still* go and marry someone else outside their immediate church circle.

When you are in a religious environment and you ask men which qualities they want in a woman, you will hear cliché answers, like "a God-fearing woman", "a woman who prays", "a woman who loves the Lord", etc. Ask the same men the same question in an environment where they will not be judged for being honest and practical, and you will begin to hear more honest answers in addition to their cliché responses.

Many churches are filled with spiritually empowered women, who are unfortunately bankrupt in other important areas that many men consider vital in relationships. Many churches spiritualise love to the point where many men and women are ill-prepared for marriage and are dumbfounded when they find themselves facing inevitable realities in a marriage when they *do* get married. A close look at the Bible will show you that, though marriage is a spiritual thing, it also has a lot of *practical* elements to it, and you need *both* aspects to succeed in a relationship.

Here are a few points some men I have interacted with and counselled have raised about finding a Christian woman to marry:

Social skills: Many single men emphasised that a lot of church ladies lack the social skills to engage with them outside the church setting. Effective communication, active listening, respect, open-mindedness and conflict resolution are some of social skills people need in order to build a healthy relationship. However spiritual you are, if you lack these tools, you might attract people but be unable to retain them, or you might even repel people. A number of single sisters spend so much time in church and in religious environments, they are unable to successfully function in a non-religious environment, or in places where Christians and non-Christians do everyday life. Being saved is not a call to isolation from the real world, but to being insulated in Christ and still function as part of the wider world. How can we reach the world if we are not in it? Yes, we are not of this world, but we live and interact with people in the world.

Fun-loving: Many men lamented the fact that some Christian women are oblivious to fun things or see fun things as either a distraction or worldly care. Holy living doesn't mean you cannot have fun! Relationships are *meant* to be fun. Spirituality is good, but if all you are going to do on dates is read the Bible, pray and go to Bible study, then you may struggle on the relationship journey. Most men I have met — including pastors, who preach about godliness, spiritual discipline, maintaining focus and other Christian virtues, etc — you would assume, when the time came, they would date or marry someone as serious and pious, but no. They usually go for women they consider to be exciting and fun-loving. It isn't a sin to be fun-loving; as a matter of fact, it is a relationship booster.

Mentioning the M word on the first date: A lot of Christian women consciously or subconsciously scare men away when they use the M word prematurely. If you're meeting a man for the first time, and you are harassing him with the M word, he will most likely hold back. A lot of dedicated Christian sisters have been indoctrinated to only think and talk marriage when meeting a man. I understand the need to cut to the chase and not waste precious time, but marriages are built on *friendship,* and you should seek to become his friend first before becoming his wife.

Sex and finances: Many Christian women shy away from talking about certain key areas of marriage, like sex, finances and romance — even when they are being courted for marriage. Many wait until they are actually married before they start talking about these key areas of married life. There seems to be a taboo culture about these subjects — even in certain premarital classes. A lot of men dread waiting to find out the answers to these topics after they have tied the knot, so they tilt towards women who talk freely about these issues, and to ladies who will not judge them if they initiate these discussions. Many men desire but are afraid to talk about such matters for fear of being called carnal. Christians should be able to have a mature talk about sex without fear, stigmatisation and without committing fornication. Many Christian marriages are crashing and burning, because of issues around sex, finances and communication, and it makes a lot of sense to have an early conversation around these subjects with the person you hope to spend the rest of your life with.

Desperation: Some ladies show their desperation so much that bad men are able to take advantage of them, and some good men just get turned off by it. A number of ladies are so desperate for a relationship or marriage, they are willing to tolerate anything and everything. They meet a guy they barely know and begin to spoil him with gifts and treats, paying his bills, pampering him, etc — anything to win his approval. Desperation makes people lose their self-worth; it makes them vulnerable to people who will take unfair advantage of them. Desperation is a major turn-off for honourable men who want to have a decent and balanced relationship. It isn't a crime to show love and generosity towards someone you admire, but let it not be done out of desperation, because relationships built in and around desperation do not stand the test of time.

Unrealistic expectations: So many people are unable to enter into a relationship — or retain one — because of unrealistic expectations, and there are many reasons why people have them. In a world where marriage is often seen as an end goal, numerous people have built up these high expectations for the person they hope to marry. Unfortunately, this puts unnecessary pressure on some men, who will prefer to back out of a relationship or refuse to enter into one with anyone who puts them under what they see as the needless stress of impractical demands.

Numerous ladies are in search of 'the perfect man' even though they themselves are not perfect. They want a man with the perfect job, perfect history, perfect health, perfect spirit, perfect mind, etc, but there is no such thing as 'the perfect man'; he simply doesn't exist. There *is* such a thing as 'the *right* man', however. Every man is a right man for someone, so, just because a lady thinks a guy is not 'good enough' for *her*, doesn't mean he is not 'good enough' for someone else. Most men would rather look for a reason to exit a relationship — or not even enter into one — with a lady who makes them feel inadequate in any way. In this 'name-it-and-claim-it' generation, many sisters have developed a mindset that they can get anything they want by faith, but they fail to realise that 'faith without works is dead' (James 2:17).

Contentious or strong? Some brothers emphasised the difference between a contentious woman and a strong one. Many Christian men are attracted to strong women but are put off by those who are contentious. Some women, however, view being contentious as being strong, but no! You can be *strong* without being *contentious*. Sister, if you are always shutting him down, disagreeing with everything he says disrespectfully, or seeing him like an opponent in a boxing ring, then it won't be long before you lose him. I respect women who are strong, principled, with strong convictions, yet remain respectful of others, and many Christian men are attracted to such women.

The language of honour: Many men value ladies who honour them. This brings out the king in them, and causes them to place a high value upon such a lady. Honour should be mutual in a relationship but, unfortunately, some women automatically expect to be honoured, but struggle to show honour in return. Many single men will not demand honour — they may not even talk about it — but it matters to them and can often determine who they eventually marry. Honouring a man is one of the ways to quickly get his attention and dishonouring him one of the quickest ways to lose him. Sadly, many men don't talk about this for fear of being labelled.

Mentorship: Everyone who is preparing or hoping to get married already has a mindset about marriage, about the role of parties in a relationship, and the kind of relationship they hope to build for themselves. The question is, where or who did they get this mindset from? Who is teaching our church sisters about men? Who is teaching them how to relate, engage and interface with men? Sadly, many Christian sisters have learnt about men from other women, women who have either been betrayed or abandoned by men. Some get mentored by bitter and angry women, who in turn raise suspicious and bitter mentees, creating a vicious circle of women who know little or nothing about men. The best person to teach you about men is a man. Unfortunately, many single sisters may have grown up in a home where the man was either absent or inactive, so they automatically had to listen and work with what they were being told by the women in their lives, based on their own experiences of other men.

The impact of a present and active father on his daughter cannot be understated; it has an effect that will live with the daughter for a lifetime. In the same vein, the chances of a lady, without any male figure in her life, learning honest truths about men is so slim. This doesn't mean, however, that a lady without a male figure in her life cannot have a successful relationship. Regardless of your life's experience, you can still build a solid relationship with God on your side.

These are some of the points many men have raised with me over the years as being the reasons they struggle to find a good Christian woman to marry. However, there are other inherent reasons for this struggle: fear of commitment, fear of failing and fear of rejection are genuine reasons some men give. Another observation I have made, on the side of some single Christian men, is they either don't tend to communicate the real reason(s), and withdraw from a relationship, or they don't give any reason at all; they just ghost the sisters, making them wonder why the relationship didn't take off or take root.

When a man begins to tell a lady he is in a relationship with things like "You are too good for me", "You deserve someone better", "The problem is not you, it's me", "I'm not ready yet, I need more time", etc, the chances are, the real reason for halting or exiting that relationship goes far deeper than what is being said. Brother, don't ghost a sister. Show her respect, and communicate your concerns to her and, if you must end the relationship, you need to do so respectfully.

Sister, for every man there is a woman, and for every woman there is a man. It doesn't matter if women outnumber men globally, God has designed a way of making the right people cross paths and find each other. I hear a lot of women complain about not having enough single men in their church or circle, but don't put God in a box. Serving God requires faith. God is not moved by statistics. I have seen God bring couples together miraculously over and over again. If God can do it for one, He can do it for another. Even if it looks as though nothing is happening right now in your love life, God is working behind the scenes in your favour, just trust Him. If you desire to be married, and you commit your ways to the Lord, He will direct your path. The Scripture says: "The Lord directs the steps of the godly, He delights in every detail of their lives" (Psalm 37:23 NLT). God doesn't just love you, He delights in every detail of your life, including your love life.

Brother, God delights in every detail of your life, too. Finding the right woman can be a real struggle if you want to do it all by all yourself, but you need God's help. We serve a God who sees the end from the very beginning, so it's wise to commit your future into the hands of the One who knows what the future holds. Regardless of your intellect, wisdom, exposure and expertise, when it comes to finding the right woman, as a man, you need God. Not every good woman is meant for you; there is a good woman out there who is suitable for *you*, a woman who will add value to *your* life and be a companion who will bring *you* fulfilment on the journey of life — a woman who will bring you so much favour when you find her, as the Scripture says: 'The man who finds a wife finds a treasure, and receives favour from the Lord' (Proverbs 18:22 NLT). Don't listen to naysayers; there are a lot of good Christian women out there, and I believe some of the best wives in the world are Christian women.

Are you waiting to be found by your soulmate, or are you searching for your soulmate? Someone is out there praying to meet you. May your paths cross, and may you find true love that will last forever.

INFORMATION ABOUT THE WRITER

Abraham A Jones is an author and teacher of the Word with over 20 years of experience in leadership in various capacities.

He is the coordinator of Kingdom Relationships, Head-Start classes, Connect Conferences, and Fresh Fire Conferences — forums aimed at equipping believers, empowering singles, strengthening relationships, and helping people find true fulfilment in life as designed by God from the very beginning.

Abraham is married to Kim and they currently reside in the United Kingdom.

To connect with Abraham visit www.kingdomrelationships.com or www.abrahamjones.com

Email: aaj.official.com@gmail.com

THE CURSE OF ENFORCED SINGLENESS IN THE CHURCH

by Pastor Dave Daniel

The first thing I need to do is qualify the alarming heading I have chosen to name this chapter with.

I want to be clear: in no way am I insinuating that being single and a Christian is a curse. Indeed, some people have been blessed by the Lord with the status of singleness. They have enjoyed it, are at peace in it, and actually consider being single as a gift from God. The apostle Paul also affirmed the state of being single as a positive way of living. He points out that being single allows the believer to serve God without distraction, and that's a good thing (1 Corinthians 7:32-35). For sure, it is without any doubt whatsoever that being single is *not* a curse.

What I *did* have a problem with, though, was the enforced state of singleness which was prevalent in many of the churches I knew of and had been associated with — and sadly, the church to which I was pastor.

A bit of context

In 1993, we completely demolished our church building, and finished the rebuilding project in the summer of 1996. After the launch and rededication of the new building, we could sense a wave of excitement buzzing around our church. The redevelopment of church buildings — from scratch — was not a usual activity in those days. It was an amazing act of faith from those in our congregation who remained with us and saw the project through. This accomplishment drew a great deal of interest from other believers, and our church started to see the number of attendees increase almost overnight.

I was ordained as a pastor to our church, The People's Christian Fellowship (PCF) — the same church I had attended my whole life. This was 1997, the year after the completion of my degree in Theology.

There was a strong sense of unity within the congregation at that time. And, after the millennium, we initiated some very exciting projects, such as the inception of house groups, our very own Bible Academy, a homeless persons' ministry, plus our church choir was acquiring a very good reputation in the gospel music field, which raised its profile. Many new attendees testified to the fact that our church choir was one of the main reasons they were attracted to our church, and those were the days when the choir sang at every Sunday morning service. Being at PCF was exciting, and our attendance numbers were steadily increasing.

The Issue

I noticed that, in our church, we had what I could only describe as some of the most beautiful Christian women, who truly loved the Lord and who were wholeheartedly committed to Him and to the work of His Church.

Women were in the majority within our church, as was the case in so many other ministries. Many of these women were well educated and had good careers; some had invested in their own property, were running their own businesses and, I personally felt, would make great wives, especially considering their relationship with the Lord.

Then came for me the gradually intense and disheartening realisation that, had these wonderful sisters not been in the church, and had they not chosen to live by the standards that our church had set out, they would more than likely have been in some kind of intimate relationship, or at least had more opportunities to establish friendships with prospective partners outside the church community.

The standard

Whether it was cultural or historical matters not, but our church — a Black-majority church — held matters of holiness and the inerrancy of the Holy Bible in high regard, and we still do today. This meant that our lifestyle practices had to be filtered through our understanding of what we believed God's Word allowed.

One of those standards of expectation was the belief that believers should only be involved in intimate relationships with other believers (1 Corinthians 7:3, 2 Corinthians 6:14), and that sexual intimacy could only be expressed within the confines of the marital union (1 Corinthians 7:2, Hebrews 13:4).

There simply weren't enough eligible single men to match the number of single women who attended PCF; they were outnumbered by far. Yes, the church was busy; it was exciting; there were many interesting things to get involved in; we were beginning to make our mark in the community; we had an established prison ministry, and the functionality of all these great things happened only because our church fellowship was committed to the work.

But what about the future? What hope did the single people in our church have of forming relationships, which could and should result in marriage and the possibility of producing a family? The few men who attended our church were spoilt for choice, and I emphasise the word 'few'. The situation for the women, on the other hand, was horrifyingly bleak.

I remember something else that troubled me: the sorry statistic which revealed that within our congregation we had rarely even seen a boyfriend or girlfriend relationship materialise for a considerable length of time.

The concept of dating was looking more and more like some prehistoric phenomenon. On the surface, our sisters seemed to be coping; there was this hopeful dream, an unspoken desire that something would someday change, and we would all live happily ever after, but nothing was being done to address the situation. Faith is absolutely awesome, but without works, the Bible states, it is dead (James 2:26).

Things had to change

We failed to address some of our practical and challenging matters seriously. We preferred to exist in a Christian sphere of happiness, overflowing with victory and supernatural joy. However, our Bible is totally balanced. On the one hand, it appears to present a utopia-like Christian experience where all you need is faith to unlock the most enviable state of happiness. But, on the other, it also addresses the reality of life's challenges: bad things can happen to God's people over an extended period of time and for a variety of reasons. Unfortunately, we seemed to prefer to focus on the blessings, rather than address the negatives which were sometimes staring us right in the face.

This is how we dealt with the enforced single issue in our church. We didn't need to talk about it, "Just keep the faith" and "God would make a way". But really and truly, this approach is what we needed to change. The phrase, "I agree" may have made us feel a bit uncomfortable at times, but we had to call out the issue of *enforced singleness* for what it truly was: it was a curse.

I found it terribly difficult to accept that this was God's plan or His intentional will for His children; that, as soon as a person becomes a believer, the chances of developing relationships with the opposite sex became — in the main — unachievable. The only reason why there weren't any blossoming relationships in our church at that time was because they were statistically almost impossible to birth. I noticed the same issues we were facing were prevalent across many churches: there were more females and simply not enough men, and so relationships were just not happening as they should have been.

What I have just described is very different from *choosing* singleness or being blessed with that status by the Lord. I noticed there were many people who would have loved to be in a relationship, but by virtue of being in the church, that option now became non-existent. I could not and would not accept this as being God's will.

What we did

We were persistent in addressing this situation, which we believed wasn't pleasing to God. It was also our firm belief that the Lord had chosen this season to be the one where we confronted this challenge to His Church. Head on.

Suddenly, the curse of enforced singleness was on every prayer list. We asked God to provide us with a miracle, to change the current trend, to ready our hearts for the change. Prayer was at the foundation of our approach to this issue. The mothers and fathers of our church were praying, and many of us were believing… We'll come back to the point of believing a little later on.

The narrative in our church fellowship started to change. A number of activities were purposefully introduced to encourage a change of perspective.

Surprisingly, some of the very women whom I believed would benefit from us highlighting this situation — with the expectant result that change would occur — provided me personally with the greatest opposition.

I remember asking the Women's Ministry leader whether she would allow me to come to one of their meetings to talk about the problem of enforced singleness in our church, and to express my confidence that, with God's help, we could see a change. I certainly didn't have all the answers. I didn't know how things could or would change, but I had faith in that specific word from the Lord: that if we regularly addressed the situation by exposing it for what it was, then our perspective would change, and our persistence could create an atmosphere of expectation and new possibilities.

At the end of the meeting, I remember standing with my back against the wall, being surrounded by a group of young adults who were questioning me — with some force. They just couldn't see how all this talk was going to change anything. Plus, some of them must have felt I was the wrong person to broach this subject, especially seeing that I was a married man, and couldn't possibly relate to their experience. I thought at the time that their reaction was actually a result of deeper hurts which were now being uncovered.

I eventually got out of that meeting unscathed but will never forget the way those dear sisters responded. Needless to say, despite that experience, I wasn't perturbed, and continued with the mission of exposure, but now with even more fatherly audacity.

Some of our Sunday evening services were taken over by a special programme, which we entitled the 'Relationship Forum'. These sessions took place at least once a quarter. The sole purpose of this forum was again to inflame the faith of the congregation and create a churchwide atmosphere of expectation. We tackled the issues of Christocentric dating, even though dating was non-existent at that time. We talked about the things that would make a marriage successful. But more than anything else, I wanted the congregation to believe, dream and prepare for this ungodly situation to come to an end.

If we taught the congregation how to date in a way which honours the Lord, then we were complying with our call of pastoral care, and practically exercising our faith in God's Word for that season. Looking back at some of my teaching notes from 2004, I can see some naivety in some of the concepts I was suggesting, but it was necessary to promote a different kind of expectation for Christians to pursue when on that journey of developing friendships with persons of the opposite sex.

We had some incredibly fun sessions as well. One such occasion saw us transform the sanctuary into a courthouse. I was the King's Counsel for the defence, and I had to defend what I called 'The New Principle' for Christian dating. The prosecution was headed by one of our deacons, who argued against this alternative approach and for the more traditional organic way for developing relationships.

It was a lighthearted event, which urged the church to discuss things they had not seen but of which they were now entertaining the possibility.

Our ministry was relentless and intentional in this matter and — may I add — audacious as well. My wife and I put on a special Valentine's meal and instructed all the 'single' men in our church to ensure that every 'single' sister received at least one or two personal invitations to attend the event at our house. There was no pressure on anyone that evening. No one was paired up or set up or anything like that; we were simply trying to rebuild the bridge between the sexes in our church, and remove the misconstrued negativity regarding the developing of healthy Christian friendships between different sexes. We hoped the circle of friendships might increase after that evening, and the suspicious defensive barriers, that may have unconsciously been created between men and women over the years, might be removed.

We had a great evening of food, discussions and games. However, the very last two people to leave the house, several hours after the gathering was officially over, I might add, started talking with each other more regularly after the event, and began a purposeful friendship. It gave me so much joy to be the minister who married them to each other. Praise the Lord, something was happening.

The miracle

I had and still have an incredible relationship with the PCF choir. They know how I can be a little bit mischievous at times. So, I tried some things with my choir, which I would never advise anyone else to copy.

The choir had been working on an album, and we were receiving invitations to minister at various events. On occasions, I would introduce the choir members by name, and then mention their status as being 'married' or 'single'. Cheeky, I know, but it was done with a lot of humour. And yes, I may have had to rebuff one or two minuscule attitudes from a few of my singers. Yet I never heard a single complaint when they walked down the aisle to their husbands, whom they got talking to after said event. And that's it, we were now in the season of the miraculous. God's will *was* breaking through; He was making a way.

There had been about four beautiful wedding ceremonies, which I can recall happening between the completion of our church rebuild in 1996 and 2003. Then, between 2004 and 2008, we experienced the answer to our prayers in quite an unexpected and dramatic way — the Lord outpoured a unique anointing over our church. First there was one marriage, the next year there were three, the year after that there were four, then eight then four again. That's 20 marriages for a relatively medium-sized congregation of around 200 plus persons. For this to have happened over a period of five years, which is a comparatively short period of time, is nothing short of the miraculous – and we praise the Lord.

Being forced into a situation of singleness, only because you have come into relationship with Christ, cannot be right. We acknowledge that not every Christian will become married, but that shouldn't have to be our portion simply because we have now come to faith.

And why does this situation exist? There are in fact several reasons, but one very obvious reason is because of the vast imbalance of the sexes within our churches.

What next?

The question my fellow leaders and I have to address is: if we agree that the state of enforced singleness is not God's will for our congregations, what can we do? For the People's Christian Fellowship, that season was great, but still not every person in our church fellowship is or became married during that season. The frustration of enforced singleness is not necessarily lifted by this dramatic testimony alone. Persistence is required.

Compatibility and marriage readiness are personal factors that do have an effect. That one single man and that one single woman in your church may not actually be best suited to each other, so avoid enforcing a marriage between them. There could be a prospective partner in another congregation somewhere else, however. Couldn't we as ministers do more to eliminate this challenge for our congregants?

How does the message come across that, as soon as you become a follower of Christ, you are most likely going to have to accept celibacy for the rest of your life? That thought distresses me intensely.

What are the origins of this problem?

There are several reasons, I am sure, but I think it's partly because of the way in which we have allowed our churches to evolve. My gut feeling is that we, the Church, have abandoned our foremost purpose and mission, especially the one to become disciple makers and witnesses for Christ.

We have abandoned the mission and the Gospel of truth and have opted for a more emotively-driven experience. Just ask some believers to explain the Gospel of Jesus Christ, as based on the Bible, and note the variants and additions we have introduced to the concept. It is unfortunate, really. We need to understand that our emotions are extremely powerful, and they shape our expectations of what the Church should be like and should be doing.

Right next door to our church building is a betting shop. Every day it is full of men. The one thing that will change those men and move them into our churches is for them to have a similar experience to that of the Apostle Paul, whilst he was going about his business, with destructive intentions on the Damascus Road. He was arrested by the words of Christ.

Men need to hear the Gospel message, and we need to find pleasure in making disciples for Christ, but how will they hear unless someone is ready to go? This has to be our focus and our mission. This must become the matter which drives our agendas, and by God's grace, He will fill His Church and reset the balance.

INFORMATION ABOUT THE WRITER

David Daniel pastors The People's Christian Fellowship church in Tottenham, North London. He is a creative leader/teacher who has a BA degree in theology and is passionate for the Church to maintain its biblical uniqueness. Pastor David is also an award-winning gospel artist, a singer-songwriter, choir director and regularly conducts gospel music workshops throughout Europe.

You can connect with Pastor Daniel at www.facebook.com/dave.daniel.7796

Email: pastordave@tpcf.org.uk

About the Editor MARCIA DIXON MBE

Marcia Dixon MBE is one of the most well-known figures within Britain's Black Christian community due to her work as former Religious Columnist at *The Voice*, Britain's most well-known Black newspaper, and as Editor of *Keep The Faith*, the most widely distributed magazine about Britain's Black Christian community.

Ms Dixon's many years working within the Black Church arena led to her being listed in the Queen's Birthday's Honour's List in October 2020 for her 'Services to Inter-Faith Relations' for which she received an MBE.

Aside from working as a writer, Ms Dixon runs Marcia Dixon Public Relations (MD PR), which provides a range of PR services to help churches, ministries, businesses and organisations reach the Black Christian community.

Clients have included the YMCA, Wise Women Awards, the NHS, Sony Music, Angie Le Mar, BET, Street Pastors, Pentecostal Credit Union and Christian Aid.

Ms Dixon also hosts regular breakfast events for women which provide networking opportunities and information that will help them build their businesses, charities and/or achieve their professional goals. She also hosts masterclasses and runs online courses for individuals, business owners and ministry leaders who want to understand how implementing PR strategies can help them achieve their goals.

In 2010 Ms Dixon was appointed as a Faith Advisor to the British Labour Government and was a member of a panel comprised of 13 faith advisors, who acted as a 'sounding board' to advise the government on effective engagement with faith communities.

Ms Dixon has been part of Britain's Black faith community since her teens, and strongly believes that the Church is one of the Black community's greatest success stories.

Aside from her professional work, Marcia Dixon has a strong presence on social media and is known for her topical and engaging social media posts and her ability to generate debate and discussion on the issues that matter to the Black faith community.

During lockdown Ms Dixon discovered Zoom and hosted a series of discussions on popular topics. This included exploring the issue of singleness in the Church, divorce, and how to build successful relationships.

Ms Dixon is a volunteer lead member of the Black Church Domestic Abuse Forum (BCDAF), established to provide training for churches so that they can effectively support victims of domestic abuse. She also regularly supports charities that seek to address serious youth crime and has her own YouTube channel.

Visit www.marciadixonpr.co.uk for more information.